Behind the Wheel

The Romance of the Motor Car

Automobile Club Show

Richmond

17th to 24th June 1899

Catalogue   One Shilling.

Behind the Wheel

The Romance of the Motor Car

Michael J. Burgess

MICHAEL O'MARA BOOKS LIMITED

First published in Great Britain in 2000 by
Michael O'Mara Books Limited
9 Lion Yard, Tremadoc Road
London SW4 7NQ

A CIP catalogue record for this book is available
from the British Library

ISBN 1-85479-583-X

1 3 5 7 9 10 8 6 4 2

Designed and typeset by Martin Bristow

Printed and bound in Italy by L.E.G.O., Vicenza

Acknowledgements

With special thanks to David Armé, Sally Claxton
of Hamlyn/Octopus, Terry and Jenny Gosling,
Keith Long, and Steven Wines, for their help with
the illustrations.

Picture credits

Octopus Publishing Group: 15, 17, 21, 23, 44, 55
(*below*), 77, 83, 106, 107 (*below*), 111 (*below*), 125,
126, 134, 135; Dennis Alder: 34, 36, 37 (*below*);
Ian Dawson: 8, 9, 10, 11, 14, 16, 24, 25, 26, 27, 31
(*below*), 32, 33, 42, 47 (*both*), 50 (*below*), 54 (*below*), 55
(*top*), 67 (*both*), 68 (*top*), 69 (*top*), 70, 71 (*both*), 72, 73,
74, 78 (*both*), 79, 86 (*below*), 87, 107 (*top*), 127, 133,
138 (*below*); P. Durnford: 121; John Lamm: 35 (*both*),
37 (*top*), 41 (*below*), 58, 98 (*top*); Chris Linton: 86
(*top*), 88, 90; Peter Myers: 99 (*top*); Rainer W.
Schlegelmilch: 28, 29, 30, 31 (*top*), 82; Jasper
Spencer Smith: 75, 104, 111 (*top*); Nicky Wright: 48,
49, 50 (*top*), 51, 54 (*top*), 59, 76, 92, 98 (*below*), 99
(below), 103 (*top*), 120, 122, 143

Auto Express: 18, 19, 138 (*top*); British Motor
Industry Heritage Trust/Rover Group: 85 (*below*), 89
(*top*), 95, 110, 112, 113, 124, 128, 129; Chevrolet
Motor Division: 38, 39 (*both*), 40 (*both*), 41 (*top left &
right*); Citroën UK Ltd: 43 (*both*); Daimler Chrysler
Classic Archives, Stuttgart: 81, 84 (*all*); Dover
Publications Inc., New York: half-title page,
Contents page, 96, 97 (*both*); Ford Motor Co. Ltd:
56 (*all*), 57 (*both*), 60 (*below*), 61 (*below*), 62, 63
(*below*); Terry Gosling: 91; Imperial War Museum:
109 (*top*); Peugeot Talbot: 101 (*above right & below*),
102; Rolls-Royce Ltd: 108 (*both*), 109 (*below*); Rover
Group Ltd (formerly British Leyland): 21 (*both*),
125; SAAB Owners' Club of Great Britain: 114, 115
(*both*), 116 (*both*); Science Museum/Science and
Society Picture Library: 100; Skoda UK Ltd: 117
(*both*), 118, 119 (*both*); TVR Engineering: 130, 131
(*both*), 132 (*both*); Vauxhall Motors Ltd: 136 (*below*);
Volvo Car Corporation: 140, 141, 142, 144 (*both*);
Steven Wines: 139

Contents

Introduction

The motor car (or automobile, if you prefer) has arguably had more impact on the way we run our lives than any other comparable modern invention. It has changed the way we design our towns, do our shopping, take our holidays and court our loved ones.

Prior to the arrival of cheap mass-produced cars people were forced to work where public transport wanted to take them, and when it wanted to take them there. Now they can cheerfully look for work miles from where they live, and adapt their shifts to suit themselves.

Where once only those holiday resorts served by the railways could ever hope to become popular, now almost every corner of the world is easily accessible to anyone with a car. People can visit places which, only forty years ago, it would have been almost impossible for them to see without spending comparatively vast sums.

It is little wonder, therefore, that today, with nostalgia a fast-growing business, people remember their early cars with such great affection. What person cannot honestly say they do not recall the first trip they took on their own in their first car, or the first holiday resort they went to in it? Youthful adventures in frequently battered cars long past their sell-by dates have been part of growing up for generations of youngsters.

Older readers may have fond memories of the only motor vehicle in their road or village back in the days when a car was an unusual sight, and every journey was a real adventure, when only the village doctor, vicar and possibly teacher could afford a car of any sort. Some of the more prosperous traders and shopkeepers could truly say that they had made their money when they had been able to afford to run a van, and were considered prosperous if they could run a car alongside it. Things have changed enormously since the early days of the motor car, but it is always worth remembering that one day people will be looking at Bedford Rascal vans with the same adoration they currently offer the Ford Thames and Austin A35 of yesteryear.

The purpose of this book is to tell the stories of some of those cars, and the companies - and characters - that made them. Some of the names within these pages are still commonplace, while others will stir deep memories of forgotten makes that have long since drifted into receivership. The stories behind some of the famous makes are often surprising, and I hope the book may add a few little-known details for the even the most ardent enthusiasts. A handful of the less well-known makes are also included, just to offer a little variety, and because their histories are often interesting in themselves. Companies like Alvis and Jensen were tremendously well known in their day, but today they are all but forgotten by every one except true devotees.

As is inevitable with a book of this size, the choice of which makes to include was a difficult one. Fame and popularity have, of necessity,

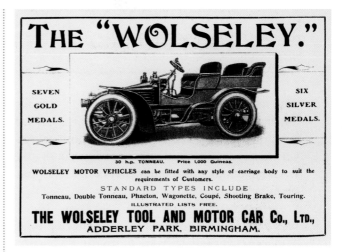

shaped the final selection, but it was not without regret that some of the smaller makes fell by the wayside. The tale of the Welsh dragon that once fronted the Gilbern range of Welsh-built sports saloons will have to wait for another volume, as will the story of the Jowett Javelin and the Bond Équipe. Had everything been included the book would have been huge, expensive and probably very boring to most people. I hope readers will find the final choice of marques reasonable, and their stories interesting.

MICHAEL J. BURGESS
May 2000

"The sixth age"

Alfa Romeo

Manufactured: 1910 to date.

The Name: The Alfa part of the name stands for Anonima Lombarda Fabbrica Automobili, which very loosely translates as Association of Lombardy Car Makers. The Romeo was added later when Nicola Romeo, a young investor, took control of the company in 1915.

The Badge: The Alfa Romeo badge is based on the coat of arms of the Visconti family of Milan. Umberto, the founder of the family, was reputed to have slain a giant serpent that was roaming the area in the fifth century AD, devouring the populace. Hence the right side of the badge shows a serpent with a person in its mouth (not sticking its tongue out as some would have you believe).

The red cross on a white field on the left side of the badge commemorates the area's involvement in the Crusades. A winner's garland seen around some examples of the badge was added in the late 1930s after Alfa Romeo won the prestigious Targa Florio races every year from 1930 to 1935.

Popular legend has it that the task of designing the badge was handed to a junior member of the design office who was inspired by the Visconti coat of arms on a major building in Milan while waiting for a tram. He reversed the design, placed it in a circle rather than a shield, and the Alfa Romeo badge was born.

History: Alfa (properly, A. L. F. A., for there was no Romeo in the early years) started life out of the remains of the Societa Italiana Automobili Darracq, the Italian branch of Darracq, a successful French car company. Despite moving the factory to be nearer the French parent company, a recession in the car market in 1908 led to the failure of Italian Darracq.

A group of car enthusiasts begged a loan from the bank that had supported Darracq and restarted production, making cars broadly based upon the ill-fated Darracq range. The first to bear the Alfa badge was the 24hp, quickly followed by a smaller 12hp model.

By 1915 A. L. F. A. was already in trouble. With funds running short Nicola Romeo was persuaded by his bank to invest in the company and add his manufacturing capacity in the engineering field.

Aside from adding his name to the company, he forced it to diversify and soon had it making

Above: The RL Super Sport tourer headed the Alfa range during the middle years of the 1920s.

Below left: A 1924 Alfa Romeo RL Type Targa Florio – the racing cars of the 1920s and 30s brought a glory that Alfa would not find again until the 1990s.

aero engines under licence from the British, railway engines, and had its car engines adapted to power trailer-mounted compressors. He also moved the company on from their early side-valve and four-cylinder engine designs. Soon they were producing up-market designs with six- and eight-cylinder engines. Double-overhead-camshaft engines with superchargers followed, as did the Bimotore, a racing car with twin eight-cylinder engines.

Guiseppe Campari gave Alfa their first racing victory in 1920, and in 1924 he drove the first purpose-built racing Alfa Romeo to victory in the French Grand Prix.

The Alfa Romeo P3 was their first single-seat racing car, quickly introduced in 1932 when the regulations forcing all cars to have an extra seat for riding mechanics were changed. It was a race-winning car from the first, and the company entered its golden age.

1925 saw Romeo forced from the board as the company was again in financial difficulties, and only the support of Benito Mussolini's government from 1933 kept the company afloat and racing. Mussolini decreed that anything which brought prestige to the name of Italy must be encouraged at all costs, and was frequently seen riding in an Alfa Romeo tourer.

Under Mussolini's funding, the Alfa Romeo racing cars designed by Vittorio Jano and managed by talented young Italian Enzo Ferrari (who would go on to produce a range of exotic cars bearing his own name) swept almost all of the opposition before them. During the 1930s Alfa Romeo managed to win no fewer than ten Mille Miglia races and four Le Mans trophies.

During the Second World War the Alfa Romeo factory was bombed three times (once after Italy had surrendered), and the company had to turn its factories to any sort of production in the immediate post-war years to keep the cash flowing. Their product range soon included domestic appliances, railway rolling stock and marine engines.

Giuseppe Farina won the first driver's World Championship in 1950 in an Alfa Romeo type

158 Alfetta. Technically a pre-war design, it had dominated the 1948 racing season and was subtly updated for 1950.

Production of road cars was slowly restarted, and took a huge leap forward in 1954 with the introduction of the Giulietta, Alfa Romeo's first mass-production car. It featured a technically advanced double-overhead-camshaft engine mated to a slick gearbox in a neatly styled bodyshell. This and other ranges of worthy sporting cars sold in large numbers all over Europe, but 1967 saw the arrival of the car that was to launch their reputation in America.

Made famous by Dustin Hoffman in the film *The Graduate*, the Spider Duetto sports car captured the imagination of the sunshine states and dreamers all over the world. Produced over the years with a wide range of engines from 1.3 to 2 litres, it remained in production for nearly thirty years. It was keenly priced, had excellent driving manners, striking good looks, and sported the famous Alfa twin-overhead-camshaft engine in an era when altogether more pedestrian engines were the order of the day

Above: The Bertone-styled GT and GT Junior models of 1966 were the first successful small Alfa Romeo cars, with production continuing until 1977.

Right: The Giulia Sprint of 1963 was the lighter, more sporting version of the Giulietta, Alfa Romeo's first mass-produced vehicle.

The engine remained the mainstay of the Alfa Romeo car range until 1971, when the car that nearly killed the company arrived. Pressed by the Italian government, Alfa Romeo opened a factory in the industrially underdeveloped and unemployment-ridden south. The result was the Alfasud (quite literally, Alfa South), a totally new design with a zippy flat-four engine and, for the first time on an Alfa, front-wheel drive. It was well appointed, featured class-leading interior space and displayed handling well beyond what anyone expected from its price. Unlike most small cars, it was actually fun to drive.

Unfortunately it also featured cheap Russian steel and was assembled by agricultural workers who would far rather have been working in the fields. The result was a car that rusted and fell apart at an alarming rate.

Behind the Wheel

With funds too tight to develop a new small car for the 1980s the Alfasud grew into the 33, which soldiered on into the 1990s in the face of falling sales.

1985 saw the introduction of the 75 saloon to commemorate seventy-five years of Alfa Romeo. In true Alfa Romeo fashion it received mixed reviews from the motoring press for its styling and idiosyncratic interior features (the electric window switches were mounted above the rear-view mirror and the handbrake was a thick metal hoop that soon earned itself the nickname 'power-station shutdown lever').

Alfa Romeo was taken over by the Fiat group in 1986 in the face of mounting debts. The arrival of the 164 saloon with its new V6 engine and its rave reviews in the motoring press came too late to keep the company independent.

Fiat have since kept all their new Alfa Romeo models true to the spirit of the originals. Against all expectations the Alfa Romeo racing team stormed to victory in the British Touring Car race series on their first outing, and their road car range continues to enjoy a healthy reputation around the world.

Is That Really True?

Henry Ford once said: 'Every time I see an Alfa Romeo go past, I raise my hat.'

The green four-leafed clover now used as the symbol of the high-performance versions of Alfa Romeo cars originated in the racing days of the 1930s. It was painted on the cars' bonnets to bring luck.

During the 1980s Alfa Romeo briefly built a car based on the Nissan Cherry, mating the running gear of the Alfasud with the Cherry body shell. It was sold as the Arna, or Alfa Romeo Nissan Automobile. Some black examples came with bright green upholstery!

Alvis

Manufactured: 1920 to 1967

The Name: No one seems to know exactly where the Alvis name came from, but the most widely held opinion is that it is a mixture of two words: 'al' for aluminum and *vis*, which is Latin for power or strength.

The Badge: The badge is a simple 'Alvis' legend set in a red triangle. However, during the 1930s Alvis became famous for their hare mascots. Featuring an alert-looking hare, they originated in the marketing phrase 'The hare ahead of the hounds', and soon became a regular feature on Alvis cars.

History: Alvis started life as TG John Ltd, whose first car, the 10/30, was unremarkable and hinted little at what was to come. By the time car pro-duction was called to a halt in 1967, Alvis had become famous in the fields of car, military and aero engineering.

The 10/30 was named in the English tradition of the time. The first number was the car's nominal RAC horsepower rating for tax purposes, and the second number was the actual bhp produced by the vehicle's engine.

In time the 10/30 was refined into what was to become one of the greats of the 1920s, the 12/50 tourer. A smooth, refined touring car with a surprising turn of speed, it was developed into the 12/60 for the 1931 season and by the standards of the day offered remarkably comfortable and rapid transport.

Between 1928 and 1930 Alvis experimented with a supercharged 1-litre eight-cylinder competition car that was the world's first front-wheel-drive car to feature fully independent suspension. A range of road cars was launched based on this vehicle. Technically ahead of their

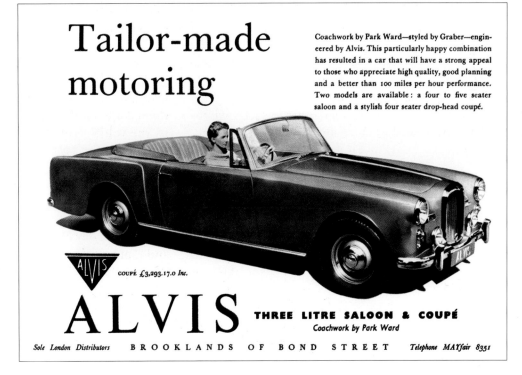

Tailor-made motoring

Coachwork by Park Ward—styled by Graber—engineered by Alvis. This particularly happy combination has resulted in a car that will have a strong appeal to those who appreciate high quality, good planning and a better than 100 miles per hour performance. Two models are available: a four to five seater saloon and a stylish four seater drop-head coupé.

ALVIS

COUPÉ £3,293.17.0 Inc.

ALVIS

THREE LITRE SALOON & COUPÉ
Coachwork by Park Ward

Sole London Distributors BROOKLANDS OF BOND STREET *Telephone* MAYfair 8351

time, they were too expensive to sell well and the range was quietly discontinued in 1930, allowing Alvis to concentrate on the better-selling touring cars.

A six-cylinder engine was developed for 1927 and fitted to a 12/50 chassis to create the 14/75, the sort of car Alvis would become famous for. In direct competition with the likes of Bentley, the soon renamed Silver Eagle was given a new 2-litre engine for 1933 to create a faster model called the Crested Eagle. All these cars were supplied with suitably styled bonnet mascots that would never make it through today's safety regulations, but which made the cars an imposing sight on the road.

The small sports-car market was not neglected as the smaller 1.5-litre Firefly was launched in 1932, joined by the Firebird in 1933 to fight for the sales of companies like MG.

TG John met Charles Follett by chance, and Follett's agreement to take a third of Alvis's production led to the development of the beautiful Speed models of the late 1930s. Leading the range was the Speed Twenty, which was available in a number of body styles, with any of which

the car could manage 90mph. A Speed Twenty-Five quickly followed with a 3-litre engine and a top speed of 95mph. Last of the group was the new Speed Twenty-Five, fitted with an enlarged 4.3-litre engine to produce the first Alvis to offer a top speed of 100mph.

All of the Speed range offered fast, luxurious touring for the wealthy gentleman of the time. Their body styles were all fashionably up to date, and many enthusiasts would argue that they have never been bettered. Certainly they represented the peak of the Alvis name.

During the Second World War Alvis turned to military production, and with the return of peace it was deemed unwise to relaunch the mighty 4.3-litre into the depressed market. Instead the company chose to restyle and relaunch its small 12/70 line, which had been seen briefly before war broke out as the TA14. Although once again a well-mannered car available in a wide range of body styles, it could not be described as fast. The sports-car enthusiasts were catered for by the TB14, a controversially styled open two-seater that probably suits today's taste better than that of its own era.

Alvis

1950 saw the arrival of the new six-cylinder engine in the TA21. Faster than the other post-war cars, it was still a far cry from the stylish cars that had run through the 1930s. The TB14 was also fitted with the new engine to create the TB21, a faster but still unloved sports car fighting a losing battle in the Jaguar XK price range.

In 1953 the last of the Alvises styled in-house was launched in the form of the TC21/100, better remembered as the Grey Lady. A 100mph saloon, it was recognizable from the earlier TA21 range by the presence of a pair of rather strangely styled bonnet air scoops and its centre-lock wheels. It would last until 1955, by when new designs were in the pipeline.

The Swiss car stylist Graber had exhibited a grand touring car on an Alvis chassis around the motor shows of 1951 to much acclaim. It featured a tastefully updated radiator grille and rounded lines much more in keeping with the times than the flat sides of the Grey Lady. A new six-cylinder

engine was fitted and the whole car launched as the TD21 in 1956.

As time passed, the car gained better brakes, still more power and a number of small styling tweaks. Convertibles became available, and the bodywork was constructed by a number of external coachbuilders to keep pace with the demand.

The glory days of the fast open tourer had returned for Alvis, if only for a short time. The TF21 of 1964 featured the ultimate development of the Graber cars with a new four-headlight treatment of the nose styling and an even more luxurious interior. By now the engine featured no fewer than three carburettors, and the car could reach 120mph.

Rover took a keen interest in Alvis as they were making cars that came very close to the market they were targeting with their P5 3-litre range, and in 1965 they bought the rival company. Car production ceased in 1967, and the great Alvis touring-car range came to an end. The name lived on, however – indeed, some would say on vehicles more suited to today's city streets, for Alvis now concentrates on building armoured vehicles.

Before Rover took over, Alvis had been working on its next generation of cars. Alec Issigonis, who would go on to design the famous Mini, had designed a V8-engined vehicle that made use of many of the technical developments he would eventually use in his famous minicar.

Is That Really True?

When the TB14 was launched at the 1948 Motor Show it sported a door-mounted cocktail cabinet. Unfortunately this useful little feature did not make it through to the production models.

Aston Martin

Manufactured: 1922 to date.

The Name: The name Aston Martin derives from two sources. The Aston part comes from the Aston Clinton Hill Climb venue, while Martin comes from Lionel Martin who designed the first cars. Martin had had his first competition successes at this hill climb and chose to immortalize it in the name of his new car design.

The Badge: The Aston Martin name is displayed within a set of wings.

History: While the first production car was launched in 1922, the actual Aston Martin story goes back to 1913. The first car to bear the name was a competition special, powered by a Coventry-Simplex engine in an Isotta-Fraschini chassis.

A number of competition cars were the first Aston Martins produced, all based on developments of that first design. One notable buyer was the famous Count Louis Zborowski, who would go on to build the Chitty Chitty Bang Bang grand prix cars. All the cars featured a 1.5-litre Coventry-Simplex engine and the unusual refinement of front-wheel brakes. Popular thinking of the day discouraged their use because experts thought they would make the car unstable when braking from high speeds.

In 1924, Aston Martin was forced into receivership as the competition cars were not making sufficient profit. Renwick and Bertelli Engineering of Birmingham purchased the company and launched their first car in 1927. This new design made use of a 10hp engine which Bertelli had designed for the stillborn Enfield-Allday car company. Production was moved to Feltham in Middlesex before Renwick withdrew his funding and left Bertelli struggling.

The Rudge-Whitworth Cup was won by one of these new Aston Martins at the 1928 Le Mans, but production of the road cars struggled to reach twenty before financial difficulties set in. The cost of the extensive racing programme was crippling an otherwise viable company. The company changed hands again in 1931, the new owners being London car dealer Lance Prideaux-Brune and financier R Gordon Sutherland.

A mixture of Bertelli's skills and Sutherland's money brought a string of competition wins in the 1930s. The 1.5-litre engine was replaced in 1936 by a more powerful 2-litre twin-overhead-camshaft unit, again designed by Bertelli. The engine was then put to use in a handsome range of two-seater sports and saloon cars until the Second World War interrupted production.

Above left: The Alvis 'Speed' models of the late 1930s, inspired by Charles Follett, were the first to offer a genuine 100mph top speed. This is a 1939 Speed Twenty-Five.

Right: The DB3S was a purely racing design primarily intended to bring Aston Martin the prestige of success on the race track; its successor, the DBR1, took the Sports Car Championship in 1959.

In 1947, David Brown of tractor manufacturing fame purchased Aston Martin after answering a newspaper advertisement offering a car company for sale and inviting bids. He developed a new car which he named the DB1. In using his initials as part of the car's name he started a line of names that would still be in use in the 1990s.

Almost at once Brown proceeded to purchase the ailing Lagonda car company and make use of its WO Bentley-designed straight-six engine in the DB1 to create the DB2 of 1950. An uprated DB3 quickly followed, and in 1955 the entire company moved to a new factory in Newport Pagnell, Buckinghamshire. All the early DB cars offered rapid performance in a grand-touring rather than an outright sporting style, with a tuned Vantage version available from 1951.

David Brown shared his predecessors' taste for racing, and the DB3S was developed to bring some trophies home to the factory. This handsome open roadster developed no less than 210 bhp at a time when the Vantage road cars were still producing 120 bhp. Rapid development led eventually to the DBR (for racing)1 which took the 1959 Sports Car Championship.

The most famous of all the Aston Martin ranges saw the light of day in 1959. The entire method of construction was changed. Gone was the old chassis-construction method, and in its place Aston Martin adopted the Superleggera construction system. Under this, the frame of the car is made up of a skeleton of metal tubes welded together to form a framework. The body and other components are all hung on this frame to create a light but very rigid structure. The new car wore a sleek fastback body and was known as the DB4; it was quickly followed by the similarly styled DB5 and 6 models. All were sumptuously equipped cars capable of covering vast distances in complete comfort at highly illegal speeds.

The shape was made doubly famous from 1964 by the car's use in the James Bond films *Goldfinger* and *Thunderball*. That silver-grey DB5 has been dubbed the most famous car in the world, and even today having an Aston Martin DB4/5/6 in silver-grey adds to its price over a similar car in a different colour.

Engine sizes started at 3.7 litres for the DB4, and grew to a full 4 litres for the later DB5/6/S models, all with six cylinders. Even the smallest offered effortless performance and vivid acceleration for the well-off driver.

The last of the family, the DBS, gained a new 5.3-litre V8 engine for 1969, but development costs had been high for the small company. Financial difficulties hit hard yet again in 1974 when Aston Martin set about cleaning the engine's emissions to make it acceptable for the American and Canadian markets. As a result, Canadian Rolls-Royce dealer George Minden and American Peter Sprague brought the company, but by 1981 it had passed into the hands of Victor Gauntlett of Pace Petroleum.

Tickford coachbuilders had been added to the group by David Brown, but he made little of the famous name within the Aston Martin range. This was quickly to change. Gauntlett soon had the coachbuilders turning out up-market versions of mass-produced cars alongside the Aston Martins. Ford Capris and Austin Metros were among the cars to get the Tickford luxury treatment, and thus a whole new generation came to hear of one of the founding names of the British motor trade.

The 1980 Motor Show featured a remarkable one-off Aston Martin called the Bulldog which had gull-wing doors and such modern gimmicks as a rear-view television camera and a built-in loud-hailer. Brilliantly styled, it was said to be able to touch 180mph, with power coming from

Behind the Wheel

a mid-mounted version of the usual V8 engine. It still exists, and the current owner has reputedly turned down an offer of over £1 million for it.

Gauntlett rationalized the range for the 1980s and had production concentrated on three vehicles: the Vantage V8, its Volante convertible sister, and the vast luxury Lagonda. Designed by William Towns, the Lagonda was a worthy successor to the Lagondas of old, offering seating for four at any speed you chose up to and well beyond the legal limit anywhere. Designed to make use of all the refinements the time could offer, the Lagonda (by now a model rather than a make) was fitted with instrument displays on TV screens in place of the usual dials, proximity switches that did not actually move when operated and just about every automatic gadget imaginable.

Ford took control of Aston Martin in 1987, to cries of horror from enthusiasts everywhere. How could such a large company hope to lavish enough care on such a small, specialist company? They were soon answered.

The whole V8 range was replaced by the Virage in 1988, closely followed by an open Volante version. The old V8 engine gained four valves per cylinder head to raise the power output. Demands for a range-topping performance version to beat the likes of Ferrari were answered in 1992 with the launch of the twin-supercharged 550bhp Vantage. Capable of 180mph, the Vantage answered all its critics. People began to think that maybe Ford money would not be so bad for Aston Martin after all.

A new 'budget' Aston Martin was launched in 1993, and the old naming traditions were restored as it was christened the DB7. Open versions were available from 1996, and a new V12 engine has recently joined the range. Aston Martin looks set to start the new century on a high.

Above left: The 1970s DBS V8 was a logical development of the earlier DB models, using the new V8 engine rather than the ageing straight-6 unit whose origins went back to the Lagonda company.

Right: The fabulous Lagonda of 1976 showcased just about every electronic gadget, including TV-screen instruments and proximity switches.

Audi

Manufactured: 1910–1939; subsequently 1965 to date.

The Name: The company was formed by Dr August Horch of Germany. His original company was called Horch Werke, and when he moved on to form another car company he called it Audi Werke. *Horchen* (an approximation of his name) is German for 'to listen', and Audi derives from Latin *audire*, meaning the same.

The Badge: The modern Audi badge is made up of four interlocked rings. This represents the amalgamation of the four companies that were formed into the Auto Union group in 1931 – Audi, Horch, DKW and Wanderer.

History: Dr August Horch was already well known for a range of cars that bore his name when he started his second car business in 1910. His first car produced under the Audi brand was the Type B, a sporting touring design (quite what happened to the Type A is a mystery).

He entered the Type B in the 1911 Austrian Alpine Trial with a team of his factory mechanics, with some success. The cars completed the event without any penalties, and went on to do the same again in 1912. A third attempt in 1913

saw the team actually win the event in their new Type C. From then on the Type C became known as the Alpine Victor.

Types D and E were briefly produced before the First World War stopped all production in 1914. The Type C chassis was reinforced and used as a basis for military trucks to help the war effort.

The earlier models were reintroduced after the Armistice, but by now Horch had lost interest in the company after being forced to limit himself to military designs, and moved on in 1920. The successful Type C was superseded by the Type G for the 1922 season, and design work started on a range of up-market six- and eight-cylinder cars for 1924.

The mighty 3.5-litre eight-cylinder Imperator (or Type K) of 1928 was the high point of Audi design. It was a big grand-tourer in the European tradition of Bentley or Alvis, capable of allowing its occupants to cover ground quickly in total comfort.

The same year also saw a change of direction for Audi as there was a change of ownership. From now on the company would spend much of its time assembling mixtures of components from other manufacturers rather than building its own cars.

The new owner, JS Rasmussen, bought the rights to assemble American Rickenbacker engines in Germany, and from then on many Audi vehicles made use of them.

The first new car arrived in 1931 in the form of a small 1.1-litre vehicle using a Peugeot engine fitted to a DKW chassis. Audi had now become part of the great German Auto Union combine (alongside DKW, Wanderer and Horch), which effectively encompassed most of the German motor industry. As BMC would do in Great Britain in the 1950s, engines and parts were juggled to produce as wide a range of cars as possible at a minimum outlay to the company.

To that end the Audi name was given to a selection of Wanderer-engined front-wheel-drive cars in the late 1930s. The finest of these was the Type 225, a large, graceful touring car in the classic Audi mould.

Below left: Early Audi models were often aimed at the wealthy, chauffeur-employing classes, as the partition between driver and passenger in this model demonstrates.

Right: The Audi factory made DKW cars before the latter company's name was allowed to lapse. These compact vehicles used small 2-stroke engines and were the first production cars to employ front-wheel drive and transverse engines – a system the Mini would make famous in 1959.

After the war Auto Union was nationalized in Germany, and Audi factories were put to use building small DKW-based cars before the Audi name was allowed to lapse into disuse. Mercedes-Benz gained control of the company in 1949, but it was not until VW gained a majority shareholding in the early 1960s that a new Audi was launched.

The new car was the small front-wheel-drive range called the 60 (more up-market versions were known as the 70/80 and Super 90). Based on a Wanderer floorpan, it was an unexpected sales success from its launch in 1965, and for 1968 it was joined by the larger 100 model. The millionth Audi was built in 1973, not long after a merger with the ailing NSU group, brought to its knees by its advanced but troublesome rotary-engined cars.

A sporty 100 Coupé was launched in 1969, and the range was regularly updated during the course of the 1970s. By now seen as the up-market brand of the VW company, an abrupt change was just around the corner.

Five-cylinder engines and turbochargers arrived in 1980, and in 1981 came the Audi Quattro. Fitted with a 2.3-litre five-cylinder engine, the Quattro would set the pace for a whole new generation of rally cars. Where before the debate had been between whether front- or rear-wheel drive was better in rough conditions, the Quattro used four-wheel drive and rewrote the whole rule book. Factory cars took first and second place in the 1983 RAC Rally, and went on to win just about every rally they entered until the competition managed to catch up with them. Single-handedly Audi had made nearly every works rally car obsolete overnight, leading to the development of such classics as the Lancia Integrale S4 and Metro 6R4 before an abrupt change in FIA rules made them all obsolete.

Today Audi cars continue to be developed as a range of quality vehicles marketed above those of the VW group, with great effect.

Is That Really True?

The 1981 Audi Quattro was famous for many things: powerful performance, turbo lag, slightly strange-feeling brakes, and a talking dashboard. Most owners were not amused by a car that talked to them.

The Audi factory at Zwickau was in the Russian zone of Germany after the Second World War, and up until recently produced the Trabant car, famous for having a body made of compressed cardboard.

Austin

Manufactured: 1906 to 1989

The Name: The cars were named after the company's founder, Herbert Austin.

The Badge: Early Austins display a winged-wheel design, with a steering wheel above a wheel viewed from the front. After the Second World War they wore a flying 'A' mascot on their bonnet (it also doubled as the bonnet release) and a cheerful chrome logo stating 'Austin of England'.

History: Herbert Austin was already involved in the motor trade before he started producing the cars that bore his own name. He was employed at Wolseley (with which his own company would eventually be linked) to design a car for them.

After a falling out with Wolseley, Austin designed and built his first car in 1906. Produced at the Longbridge works that were to be Austin's

home until the end of the company, it was, by the standards of the time, a big car. It featured a 6-litre engine and was available with either chain or shaft drive.

This early design was successful in the reliability trials of the day, winning both the Scottish Reliability Trial and the Hundred Guinea Dunlop Challenge Cup. Other versions quickly followed. New models came with a wide selection of engines, from single-cylinder units up to a mighty 9.7-litre six-cylinder engine. The most popular of these designs was the Twenty, closely followed by the Ten of 1910. The biggest of the family, called (predictably) the Thirty, came with electric lights and starter long before these were a common feature on the cars of the day.

In 1922, Austin created the car that would put his name of the motoring map for ever, and put huge parts of British society on the road. Enter the Austin Seven. Powered by a simple side-valve engine of 750cc, it could seat four adults in passable comfort as long as they were friendly and cruise happily at 45mph. The controls were considered light enough for women of the time to operate, and the mechanics were simple enough for a dedicated home enthusiast to deal with in the event of any problems. Produced in dozens of different body styles until production ceased in 1939, the Austin Seven is justifiably one of the most famous cars ever to come out of Britain.

After the First World War, Austin rationalized his range, doing away with many of his larger cars to leave just the Seven and the Twenty, with a Twelve later introduced to plug the gap in the range.

There were regular updates to engines and styles as the 1920s passed into the 1930s. Austin's designs were usually simple but tough and reliable. The Ten of 1932 saw the first use of the Cambridge name while all the other cars in the range continued to use numbers to describe themselves. The Ten remained in production all through the Second World War as the Light Utility Vehicle, affectionately known as the 'Tilly'.

After the Second World War, Austin set his sights higher. In 1947 the Sheerline and Princess range was launched in an attempt to take sales away from firms like Bentley. They were big, thirsty cars powered by lightly modified truck engines and they came with all the trimmings of the time. They were a sales failure, however, and were soon all renamed Princess and continued to be built by the famous Vanden Plas company. Later models were more closely based on their contemporary Austins and were all characterized by the fitting of big chrome grilles. One famous model, the 4-litre R, was actually powered by a Rolls-Royce engine, making it one of very few cars outside the Rolls-Royce range to be allowed to wear their badge. Popular legend has it that these 4-litre cars were eventually given out to Austin company reps when they proved too expensive to sell in the numbers hoped for.

The first new family of cars Austin offered after the war were mostly named after English

counties. At the bottom of the tree was the A40 Devon/Dorset (depending on the number of doors), closely followed by the A70 Hampshire (later Hereford) and the A90 Atlantic coupé. (The number after the 'A' for Austin was a measure of the horsepower each model produced, a system Austin would continue to use well into the 1960s.)

The Atlantic was a streamlined vehicle designed to sell in America. By American standards it was expensive, underpowered and lacked a suitable dealer network. Americans stuck with their cheap Chevrolets and Fords, and the Atlantic was soon dropped. Its engine would live again, however, in the Austin Healey 100.

Above left: The 1955 A30 Countryman; its successor, the A40 Countryman of 1958, was the world's first hatchback.

Above right: Herbert (later Lord) Austin (right), examines the clay model for the new-for-1951 Austin Seven, which was eventually sold as the A30.

Right: The 1959 launch of the world-famous Austin Mini was originally introduced as yet another new Austin Seven – an attempt to link the new design with the best-selling Austin Seven of the 1920s and 30s.

Facts on the performance of **THE NEW AUSTIN A70 HEREFORD**

THIS SALOON has an impressive performance. Its powerful 68 b.h.p. O.H.V. 4-cylinder engine takes it from rest to 50 m.p.h. in 14·9 seconds through all gears. It cruises comfortably at 65-70 m.p.h. and has a fuel consumption of 21 - 24 m.p.g. The independent front suspension, highly efficient brakes and firm, positive steering make it safe and easy to handle. The Hereford is built for roomy comfort too, and will give good service for years to come.

Figures by kind permission of 'The Autocar'

Austin of England

THE AUSTIN MOTOR COMPANY LIMITED · LONGBRIDGE · BIRMINGHAM

Left: Most of the cars in the first range Austin offered after the war were named after English counties – this is the A70 Hereford of 1951. The car was originally called the Hampshire.

Right: The Austin Mini (seen here in 1970s Clubman form) was an instant classic, bringing motoring within reach of many who would never previously have been able to afford a car.

In 1952 there came an event that would have huge repercussions for the whole UK car industry, and which many say was its undoing. In the face of falling sales and profits Morris Motors was forced into a merger with its deadly rivals at Austin to form the British Motor Corporation. The theory was that by standardizing components across both companies' ranges there would be huge cost savings and prices would fall.

The actual result was that, by and large, Austin forced Morris to adopt its engines and body designs, and both ranges became harder and harder to tell apart as the years went by. Badge engineering took the place of separate models for each make (Morris also produced MG, Wolseley and Riley cars). The principle was simple. You designed one good basic body and just changed the badges and grille to make it a different car. Occasionally the interior trim was also changed, and sometimes the state of engine tune. This all came to a head with the A60 Cambridge range of 1961-69. The same basic shape was also sold as the Morris Oxford, Wolseley 16/60, Riley 4/75 and MG Magnette. No wonder the public were confused, as each of these 'different' models was sold through separate dealership chains.

The new 'baby' Austin of 1952 was the A30, initially sold as the 'new' Austin Seven. It fea-tured the first use of the new 803cc A-series engine that would go on to power cars for nearly fifty years, and fitted a four-door saloon into the space occupied by a Rolls-Royce bonnet.

The larger cars were steadily developed to create the new Cambridge of 1954, along with the larger A50 and A90 saloons, increasing again for 1956 to give the A55, A95 and A105 models. The mighty six-cylinder Westminster was at the head of the Austin family tree and stayed there until 1968.

The small A40 Farina, named after its stylist, was launched in 1958 as a replacement for the A30 range. It would probably have faded from history had it not had one claim to fame, for in Country-man form it was the world's first hatchback.

The motoring world was turned on its head in 1959 when the Austin Mini was launched on an unsuspecting public. The full story is detailed elsewhere, but this little car revolutionized the way cars were designed. Suddenly, front-wheel drive was the thing to have.

The Mini design was stretched for the 1962 season to produce the best-selling 1100/1300 range of small family cars, again available in a wide range of makes from the same body shell (this time including a luxury version by Vanden Plas wearing the Princess name). A best-seller

Behind the Wheel

from the moment it was launched, it had all the Mini trademarks of excellent handling and lots of interior room. The 1100/1300 was still at the top of the charts when things all started to go wrong in 1973, but not before the basic design had been enlarged still further to produce the 1800/2200 range, and even a big executive version with a 3-litre engine.

The 1100/1300 (along with all its badge-engineered derivatives) was replaced with a single vehicle in 1973 – the much-maligned Austin Allegro. Early design sketches depicted a sharply styled replacement that should have carried the Austin name proudly into the 1970s. But plans to make use of engines from other models within the company forced a raising of the bonnet line, and what eventually emerged was a rounded, dumpy little car. Poor build quality quickly ruined any chances of its repeating the sales success of its forebear.

That aside, the Allegro, along with its slightly larger Maxi stablemate, were ground-breaking designs. In the days when most manufacturers were turning out basic, front-engine, rear-wheel-drive vehicles, the Austin range offered vehicles with front-wheel drive and transverse-mounted engines. The more deluxe models in both ranges offered five-speed gearboxes when four gears was the norm, and overhead-camshaft engines took the place of the simpler overhead-valve designs. Suspension was by Moulton's Hydragas system, offering a pitch- and jolt-free ride that the likes of Ford's Cortina could only dream about. There was even a range-topping Vanden Plas version, sporting a leather and walnut interior and a big

It's a small country.

chrome grille. Some people laughed at them at the time, but now all the good surviving examples are going to collectors in Japan.

The larger 1800/2200 range was replaced by the revolutionary wedge-shaped Austin Princess line in 1975. Big, luxurious and comfortable, the Princess was again let down by disastrous build quality.

The 1970s were not good years for Austin. BMC had become part of the sprawling British Leyland empire in the late 1960s, and things had gone steadily downhill. Regular strikes by militant unions brought the company to its knees, and nationalization followed. By the middle of the 1970s most of the Austin ranges had been revised, and much of the poor build quality had been attended to, but the damage had been done. Fleet sales were slow, and the poor quality of the early 1970s had allowed foreign cars to gain an unshakesable foothold in the British market.

The last of the best-selling Austin designs arrived in 1982 in the form of the Metro. Admittedly an updated Mini-based design, it would go on to become known as the car that saved British Leyland. Larger Maestro and Montego ranges followed before the Austin name was quietly dropped in 1989, as the management felt it had too many down-market connotations.

Bentley

Manufactured: 1919 to date.

The Name: The company was named after its founder, Walter Owen Bentley.

The Badge: All Bentley cars wear a form of the flying 'B' (for Bentley) badge. Some have a flat representation set on top of the radiator grille, others have it as an upright chrome mascot.

History: Walter Bentley started his engineering career at the workshops of the Great Northern Railway. The son of a wealthy family, he raced motorcycles at Brooklands and soon developed an interest in motor cars. He sold French DFP cars with his brother at a dealership in London, and soon began modifying them to make them faster. He even persuaded DFP to adopt some of his ideas before the First World War halted production.

After the war he returned to car sales with a burning ambition to design and build his own cars. Bentley Motors was formed in 1919 with a woefully small bank balance and a factory in Cricklewood, North London.

The new car was christened the 3-litre, the first time an engine size had been used to describe a British car. Bentley decided against using the usual RAC horsepower designation as most manufacturers did, as he felt this would make the car sound too small.

The technically advanced engine featured two spark plugs and four valves per cylinder and an overhead camshaft at a time when side and even sleeve valves were the norm. The gear lever was placed on the right of the driver, usually sitting on the running board, and until 1924 the cars only had rear brakes. Popular thinking at the time suggested that front brakes could lock up and flip the car end over end in high-speed situations.

The model was announced in 1919, despite the fact that no cars actually existed. While a non-

Below left: The Bentley 4.5-litre Supercharged (better known as the 'Blower Bentley') was designed to win at Le Mans. Only fifty were built, and today a seller can name his or her price for a good, original example.

Right: The powerhouse of the 'Blower Bentley'. The Amherst-Villiers super-charger between the front chassis rails created a potent sports-racing car for the rich enthusiast – though the great Ettore Bugatti described them as 'The world's fastest lorries'.

running car was exhibited at the 1919 Motor Show, the first actual working model was not delivered until late 1921. Like many car manu-facturers of the time, Bentley did not have a body department, preferring to supply a chassis for outside coachbuilders to clothe. Bentley favoured the work of Vanden Plas, but there were many other suppliers. Most remarkably, Bentley was sufficiently confident to offer his cars with a five-year warranty.

While Bentley had always thought of his cars as fast tourers, some customers wanted heavy, closed saloon bodies on their 3-litre chassis. To maintain the performance under these heavier weights Bentley launched the six-cylinder 6.5-litre model. Never one to miss an opportunity, he soon slipped a tuned version of the six-cylinder engine under a Vanden Plas tourer body to cre-ate the most successful of the racing Bentleys, the Speed Six.

Keen to keep up with the opposition, Bentley needed a new car to replace the 3-litre. He stretched the four-cylinder 3-litre engine to the same internal dimensions as the 6.5-litre and

fitted it to what was effectively the 3-litre chassis to create the 4.5-litre. If anyone mentions the styling of a 'classic' Bentley, the odds are they are thinking of a 4.5-litre wearing the stylish Vanden Plas touring bodywork.

Faced with bankruptcy in 1925, Bentley was bailed out by millionaire car enthusiast Woolf Barnato, which led to the development of the ultimate Bentley, the 4.5-litre Supercharged, better known as the 'Blower Bentley'. It was inspired by the earlier wins in the French Le Mans 24-hour race. Barnato argued that given more power he could easily win again, while Bentley objected to the use of a supercharger – he preferred to get his horsepower from using bigger engines. However, as Barnato was fund-ing the project, Bentley was in no position to object. Only fifty of this famous model were ever built, and their mystique far exceeds their rac-ing successes. Yet although the Speed Six won far more races, the Blower will always be seen as the ultimate Cricklewood Bentley.

Despite Barnato's aims, a Blower Bentley never won at Le Mans. Three-litre models won

Bentley

at the second ever race in 1924 (one had come fourth in 1923) and again in 1927, while a 4.5-litre took the flag in 1928; Speed Sixes took the trophy in both 1929 and 1930. One of the Blower Bentley's few claims to racing fame was taking the Outer Circuit lap record at Brooklands in 1931 at 138mph.

The talented group of gentleman racers who brought so much publicity to Bentley cars during the Cricklewood years were soon minor celebrities in their own right, and they became known in the press as the 'Bentley Boys'.

Bentley launched the stately 8-litre model in 1930, just in time for his already small customer base to be hit by the Great Depression, and even the quick launch of a smaller 4-litre model could not stop the company from becoming bankrupt and being quickly snapped up by Rolls-Royce.

Above: The Bentley 'S' series saloons of the 1950s and 60s proudly carried the company's reputation for grand-touring cars to a new generation of enthusiasts. This is a 1954 S2 built to US-specification.

Right: The convertible version of the 1950s Continental is seen by many as the ultimate post-Second World War Bentley.

Production was moved to Derby, and the great racing days of Bentley were over. Rolls-Royce marketed Bentleys as the 'silent sports car' rather than the powerful grand tourers they had been before. The first of the new models was the 3.5-litre, based on a tuned version of the then current 20/25 Rolls-Royce. It was quickly developed into the 4.25-litre, and briefly the Mark V saloon, before the Second World War stopped production.

After the war, Bentley moved to the Rolls-Royce factory in Crewe, and the new Bentley Mark VI was the first to be offered with a standard body shell. The mighty 'R'-type Continental of the 1950s was a last fling as their sporting character was eroded more and more with each new model, until by the 1970s only the grille set the Bentley apart from its Rolls-Royce stablemates.

All that was to change in 1982 when the Bentley Mulsanne Turbo was born. Based on the Rolls-Royce Silver Spirit, it featured uprated suspension and a turbocharged engine for which the Rolls-Royce range had no direct equivalent. 1985 saw the Mulsanne Turbo R (the R stood for road-holding) with even stiffer suspension to appeal to more sporting drivers.

A new Continental R quickly followed, as did an even faster Continental T and a smaller Brooklands model to appeal to those with thinner wallets. With Bentley firmly established as a separate marque again and sales rising it was snapped up by Volkswagen in 1998, just as it launched the BMW-engined Arnage model.

While seeking a new engine for the Arnage, Volkswagen produced the mid-engined Hunaudières supercar. Featuring a W16 engine, a luxurious interior and mind-boggling performance, the Bentley was officially a technology testbed, not a prototype. But with it the Bentley name has come full circle. The car started life as an expensive high-speed tourer with racing potential, and surely that is what Volkswagen have made again.

Is That Really True?

Modern Bentleys usually feature a blue background to their badges. This was not always so. Back in the early Cricklewood days the colour of the background indicated what style of Bentley chassis you had. Blue-label cars were the standard type, and featured the blue background. Red-label models featured a more tuned engine, and green labels indicated short-wheelbase cars with an even higher state of engine tune. All green-label cars were guaranteed to be able to reach 100mph.

Bugatti was once heard to describe Bentley cars at Le Mans as 'The world's fastest lorries'.

Perhaps the most famous Bentley driver in the UK was the fictional character John Steed of *The Avengers* TV series. Patrick Macnee, the actor who played Steed, actually drove five different examples during the course of the series.

BMW

Manufactured: 1928 to date.

The Name: BMW stands for Bayerische Motoren Werke. This translates as Bavarian Motor Works, Bavaria being where BMW's original factory was located.

The Badge: The badge represents a spinning aeroplane propeller as seen from the front. The blue and white are derived from the Bavarian state colours. The badge was chosen by BMW as they were initially known for their aeroplane engines, not their cars.

History: The BMW name first appeared in 1916 on well-respected aeroplane engines. The company soon diversified into other kinds of engines, including a particularly good flat-twin unit designed for light industrial work. A local company designed a motorcycle around this engine, and BMW decided that they would be able to make money by building one themselves. They exhibited their first motorcycle in 1922 and started a line of advanced motorcycles whose successors are still in production today.

Cars appeared on the scene in 1928 when BMW purchased the rights to build the British Austin Seven as the Dixi 3/15. With a shortage of cheap, affordable cars in most of Europe at this time, the company quickly captured a large slice of the domestic market.

Not content with just building the Dixi, the basic design was uprated for 1932. In an attempt to compete further with the larger quality cars on Germany's roads BMW prepared for some radical changes to the little Dixi for 1933.

The simple four-cylinder Austin Seven engine was extended to make a six-cylinder unit, which BMW installed in a new model called the 303. This was the first totally BMW-designed car, and was the first to feature the upright grille of two parallel ovals we still see today. The 303, however, was criticized for a lack of performance. The quicker 315 was launched in 1934, and this benefited from further modifications to create the sporting 315/1. The steeply angled rear of the vehicle's bodywork and the enclosed rear wheels set a styling pattern that would carry BMW into the war years.

The remainder of the 1930s demonstrated great advances in motoring technology that culminated in the powerful and justly famous 328

Left: A 1931 BMW DA4 Dixi. Based on the British Austin Seven, this was the first car produced by BMW.

Right: The BMW 328 of the late 1930s was a successful sports car in its day, and would go on to be used as the basis of the Bristol luxury-car range.

Behind the Whee

roadster. It featured an engine with an advanced aluminum cylinder head and a totally hydraulic braking system (a novelty in the 1930s, when most cars had at least some of their brakes worked by a cable system). So advanced was the engine that the British manufacturer Bristol made use of it, basically unaltered, for some years after the Second World War in its own range of up-market cars.

A BMW factory team entered in the 1940 Brescia Grand Prix scored a victory with a team of 328s, and Frazer-Nash in Britain built the 328 under licence for their home market before the Second World War effectively brought motoring to a halt for the duration.

After the war Germany and BMW were in ruins. The company turned its hand to building anything it could sell to make a profit. Products in its portfolio included kitchen pans, filing cabinets and even coal scuttles.

BMW the car maker made its first post-war appearance in 1951 with the 501 saloon. It was a heavy design that was powered by the pre-war six-cylinder engine. While neither sporting nor cheap it was tough, and soon found great favour with German taxi drivers. Due to material shortages the 501 followed the famous Ford Model T example and was available in any colour you wanted as long as it was black.

With Germany still in the process of rebuilding, BMW turned to the basic transportation market that had given it its first break with the Dixi, and purchased a licence to build the Isetta bubble car. To modern eyes this is a strange-looking vehicle with a teardrop-shaped body and three wheels; unlike modern practice the two wheels are at the front, not the rear. Powered by 250cc or 300cc motorcycle engines, the cars offered adequate performance and excellent fuel economy, with two-abreast seating. While not the ultimate in comfort, they did at least offer a proper steering wheel. Many of their contemporary micro-cars made do with crude rudder-style steering mechanisms.

The Isetta was exactly what the market wanted in those austere post-war years. Manufacture continued until 1963, by which time the introduction of small cars like the Mini and Hillman Imp had made production uneconomical. A stretched version with four wheels and a 600cc engine was briefly offered but was not a success, only lasting from 1957–9.

Also on their Motor Show stand in 1955, alongside the curious Isetta, was another car – the glorious 507 coupé. Fitted with an inspirational 3.2-litre light-alloy V8 engine and graceful bodywork, it was one of the most beautiful BMWs of all time. It was too expensive for the time, a flop in sales terms, but is regarded as one of those glorious mistakes of motoring history: the right car at the wrong time.

The V8 engine was fitted to other large BMWs, but what small profits the company saw were all coming from the little Isetta. Big luxury saloons were not what the depressed German market wanted. 1959 saw the introduction of the 700, a tiny saloon that used the 700cc version of the famous BMW flat-twin motorcycle engine. While still arguably a micro-car it looked and drove like a 'real' one. It quickly became the best-selling car in post-war Germany, but it was still not enough to keep BMW solvent.

The company became bankrupt in 1960, and was rescued by the Quandt brothers. They set

about a massive reorganization, and poured money into the design of the car on which all later models would be based.

Launched at the 1961 Frankfurt Motor Show, the 1500 saloon was styled by Micholetti, and aside from the famous grille, everything else was brand new. Features included a new four-cylinder engine and an advanced suspension system. A larger coupé version would gain the famous V8 from the 507 in 1962.

Other engine sizes quickly followed, and the model was revised into the 1602 range in 1966, which in turn led directly to the modern-style 3 Series range in 1975. The larger-engined saloons grew into the modern 5 Series in 1972, and 1976 saw the more powerful coupé range become the 7 Series. With periodic revisions these model titles look set to carry on into the foreseeable future. The exact model numbers adopted within each series identify what engine each car is fitted

Is That Really True?

For a time after the Second World War, the BMW plant in Eisenarch was in the Russian zone of Occupied Germany. The Russians carried on making BMWs from the tools they inherited, simply painting the blue sections of the roundel badge red and marketing them as EMWs, for Eisenarch Motoren Werke.

The BMW Isetta bubble car only had one door, and no reverse gear to satisfy licensing requirements in several countries (it could usually be driven on a motorcycle licence). This door was on the front of the vehicle, and opened outwards. There are many tales, possibly apocryphal, of people driving up to their garage walls and not being able to open the door. As there was no reverse gear they were trapped in their vehicle until someone came to release them.

with. For instance, the 518 is a 5 Series car fitted with a 1.8-litre engine, and a 730 is a 7 Series sporting a 3-litre engine.

BMW Motorsport was formed in 1972 to develop cars to satisfy BMW's sporting aspirations. A company within a company, their task was to make normal BMW models fast enough to take trophies in major race series around the world.

Their first car was named (logically) the M (for motorsport) 1, an experimental gull-winged supercar that had no place in BMW's model line-up. It eventually saw the light of day as a production car with a fibreglass bodyshell in 1981.

On a more productive note, BMW Motorsport developed tuned versions of most of the BMW range. These usually sit at the top of the model range and are badged with the series number prefixed by an 'M' (the 3-series version is called an M3 and so on).

BMW took control of Rover in 1998 to expand its operations, and also managed to gain ownership of the famous Rolls-Royce marque (quite how its rivals at Volkswagen managed to get control of Bentley, part of the same company, is one of life's mysteries). The future waits to see what

changes this will mean for BMW and its new partners, although Rover was sold in 2000.

Above left: The 315 roadster was created to silence criticisms that earlier models lacked performance. Pictured here is a 315/1 of 1935.

Above right: A 1963 BMW 1500 saloon. In 1961 it was the 1500 range that reversed the company's declining fortunes and set the basic styling for every BMW from then on.

Right: The versatile 1500 saloon gave birth to many derivatives, one of the most attractive being the convertible. This car is a 1973 British-specification 2002 Cabriolet.

Bristol

Manufactured: 1947 to date.

The Name: The Bristol company was named after the city of Bristol, where it is based.

The Badge: The crest of the city of Bristol is used as the badge of Bristol Cars.

History: Bristol aeroplanes had been well known for many years before it branched out into motor-car production in 1947. After the demands placed on manufacturing capabilities by the Second World War Bristol found itself with excess capacity and a decision was made to move into car production.

Bristol had links with AFN, the British BMW import agent, and these led to its first car being based on the pre-war BMW 328. In suitable homage to its inspiration, the first car was christened the 400 as if following on from the BMW 3 numbers.

As with all the designs that would come after, the first Bristol was an expensive, high-class machine. It was built to aircraft standards of production with a steel body over a wood frame, and was powered by a straight-six 2-litre engine based on the BMW 328 unit. Offering sprightly performance for its light weight, the engine would

go on to find fame with other small British car manufacturers such as AC, Frazer-Nash and Cooper.

Superleggera construction methods of aluminum panels over a tubular steel frame took over for 1948 with the updated 401 model. While visually it was obviously a revised version of the 400, this was the first of the 'Aerodyne' models styled in a wind tunnel for maximum efficiency and extensively tested on the long runway at the company's Filton headquarters. Although this is common design practice today, back in 1948 it was a revolutionary idea. A Bristol 401 was put through MIRA's (Motor Industry Research Association) wind tunnel in the 1980s, and it recorded a drag co-efficient better than that of most of today's designs.

A convertible (the 402) followed in 1949, and the engine was uprated for 1955 in the 403, which is regarded by enthusiasts as being the finest of the early Bristols.

The 404 was christened the 'Businessman's Express' when it was launched in 1955. It was the first Bristol to make use of the famous 'hole-in-the-wall' deeply recessed radiator grille, which, legend has it, was developed from an aeroplane air intake. The body was smoothed out and brought up to date as the original designs were starting to look dated. Nevertheless, the cars were all still exquisitely constructed, to standards that could make even Rolls-Royce shiver.

New models, the 405 and 406, followed, as did a Zagato coupé for 1960 (fewer than ten were made; Bristol drivers, it seems, just didn't want that sort of flashy car).

The car-making concern was separated from the aeroplane company in 1961 under the control of Sir George White (the man who had first suggested building cars and whose grandfather had founded the original British and Colonial Aircraft Company from which Bristol was descended in 1910) and Tony Crook; Crook would go on to take total control of the company in 1973.

There was a revolution with the new 407 of 1961. With its cars getting heavier and ever more luxurious Bristol was forced to look elsewhere for its engines. Even in its enlarged 2.2-litre form the six-cylinder engine was simply not powerful enough. The result of the search for a new engine was a Chrysler V8 that could haul the heavy car along at over 120mph. Initially used in 5.1-litre form, Bristol used successively larger versions as emissions requirements strangled the engine and the cars got heavier still.

The 408 of 1963 set the styling that still lives on today with a new grille (the 'hole in the wall' was gone) and a more rounded bodyshell.

The model numbers jumped from 411 to 603 in 1976, although the designs did not change much. Names took over from numbers in 1980 with the angular Beaufighter convertible, and the descendants of the 603 became the Britannia. This was in turn turbocharged in 1983 to create the rapid Brigand, the first British production car to wear a turbocharger as standard equipment.

Unlike most small British car manufacturers Bristol is moving steadily into the twenty-first century, able to sell all the cars it can make. They are still hand-made individual cars for the perfectionist, and long may they continue.

Below left: Bristol cars are renowned for their extensive instrumentation and luxurious interiors. Shown here is the dashboard of a 1982 Beaufighter, Bristol's later cars being named after some of the original parent company's most successful aircraft designs.

Right: The Bristol Beaufighter was styled by Zagato and offered a lift-out sunroof for open-top motoring when the weather permitted.

Cadillac

Manufactured: 1902 to date.

The Name: Cadillac was named after the French officer who founded Detroit in 1701, Antoine, Marquis de la Mothe de Cadillac.

The Badge: Early Cadillac models wore a 'Cadillac' script with a flourish underneath, while later models proudly bore de Cadillac's coat of arms.

History: The company that would become known as Cadillac started life as the Detroit Automobile Company in 1899. It was briefly known as the Henry Ford Company in 1901 when it put Ford's first design into production. Ford moved on in 1902 after clashes with the management and it was a condition of his resignation that the company be renamed, so allowing him to use his name on his future vehicles. The company, recently bought out by Henry Leland, was renamed Cadillac after the founder of Detroit.

The first Cadillac was a simple single-cylinder vehicle with minimal passenger protection, as was the fashion of the time. Four-cylinder models were launched in 1905, and the successful 30 model was launched in 1907. Leland believed in pioneering the use of precision engineering and advanced technology in his cars. This would lead to the first successful use of electric lights on a car, and the first electric self-starter in 1912 to replace the starting handle.

The success of Cadillac led to General Motors buying it out in 1908, so allowing GM to cover the upper end of the car market. Leland left to found Lincoln in 1917, but his passion for advanced technology was to remain with the company.

In 1915 the Type 51 would introduce the world's first commercial V8 engine. It offered all

Left: Early model Cadillacs, such as this 1905 Coupé (which, interestingly, is right-hand drive), barely hinted at the glories that were to come.

Above right: Cadillac was the first manufacturer to offer a V8 engine in its range – as in this 1928 341 Close-Coupled Sedan.

Below right: Big, handsome touring cars for the rich, such as this 1930 V16 All-Weather Phaeton, were a Cadillac mainstay for many years. Some of their names were almost as long as the cars themselves . . .

Behind the Whee

the refinement of the straight-sixes being used by the other manufacturers but took up far less space. It was improved for the 1923 season when a version with better inherent balance was introduced which gave birth to the infamous American 'V8-burble' exhaust note.

Earl A Thompson had developed the world's first gearbox synchromesh system as early as 1922, and after a demonstration Cadillac adopted it for the 1929 models. It did away with the need to disengage and re-engage the clutch repeatedly – double de-clutching – when changing gear. Now a silent gearchange just needed the driver to push the clutch pedal to the floor and move the relevant lever. Previously it had been necessary to re-engage the clutch with the gearbox in neutral to synchronize the speeds of the two gear shafts involved. Failing to get it exactly right led to an embarrassing, and sometimes damaging, crunch from the gears.

The Cadillac range grew to be more and more luxurious, with the range of engines growing to include V12s and even a V16 in 1930. This was the world's first production V16 engine, the car costing no less than double the price of the V8 model. Bodies became ever larger, with a range

of thirty-three different styles available for the V16.

Cadillac weathered the Great Depression through the support of the cheaper marques at General Motors, but a new chairman in 1934 forced the company forwards. New 'turret-top' body styles arrived in 1936, and under the skin there was a new V8 with the unheard-of refinement of hydraulic tappets that adjusted themselves, independent front suspension and even fully hydraulic brakes.

Before the Second World War forced Cadillac to turn its factories over to war work, it achieved

its long-term aim of overtaking Lincoln in the marketplace and becoming the premier motoring status symbol in America.

After the war, General Motors' design guru Harley Earl was given the task of changing the look of the Cadillac range so they did not resemble the lesser GM marques too closely. The result started the industry-wide trend towards vast swaths of chrome, huge bumpers and separate rear fins.

The 1948 Sedanet was the first to wear the fins, inspired by the twin tail fins found on some American fighter planes of the time. In addition, a new V8 engine for 1949 led to unexpected competition successes for Cadillac at Le Mans and the Daytona Beach speed trials.

In 1951 Cadillac dropped its cheaper models and concentrated solely on the top end of the luxury-car market. Automatic transmission became standard for 1952, and the vast Eldorado arrived in 1954. It was joined by the even greater excesses of the Eldorado Brougham of 1957, based on a concept car seen at the 1954 GM Motorama show. It was the first car to wear four

headlights in the modern sense of the term, and featured a stainless-steel roof. Air suspension gave a perfect ride, and the interior featured such 1990s features as a signal-seeking radio, central locking, electric seat adjusters with memory and an electric aerial. Ideas that did not make it into mainstream models included cigarette and tissue dispensers, built-in powder compacts, and a set of magnetic drinks containers. The Brougham sold for a fraction of what it cost to build as a loss leader, and the model only lasted two seasons.

As fashions dictated, successive Cadillacs of the 1950s and early 1960s became ever wider and lower, their fins growing longer and slimmer as the years went by. Their ride and refinement improved to the extent that they really were the ultimate luxury car on the American market, and only their sheer size stopped them being a sales success all over the world.

The fins had faded by the mid-1960s, but advanced engineering was again evident. Automatic air conditioning arrived for 1964, as did an interior-light delay switch and an automatic system that turned the headlights on and

Left: A 1929 Cadillac 341B convertible. After the V8 and V12 engines, Cadillac scored another first by using a V16 engine in its top-of-the-range vehicles.

Above right: Cadillac design of the 1940s marked the beginning of a trend towards fins that would start a worldwide fashion. Pictured is a Cadillac Fleetwood 60 Special of 1952.

Below right: Same name and designation, but a generation earlier. A Fleetwood 60 Special from 1941, showing the large separate wings and wide, square radiator grille which were a feature of the 1930s Cadillac range.

off as daylight levels required. The same year also saw the arrival of the vinyl roof, a gimmick that would spread right across the motoring world.

Front-wheel drive arrived for 1967, but the great days of Cadillac were nearly at an end. In the face of new laws for emissions and fuel economy Cadillacs started to get smaller during the 1970s. There was even a diesel model by 1978. Other hi-tech solutions to the fuel-consumption targets were V8 engines that could be run on four, six or eight cylinders, depending on road conditions, while most customers had to make do with smaller V6 and even four-cylinder engines.

By the mid-1980s Cadillac was fading as a market force in the United States in the face of foreign imports and a lack of public interest in its new small models. Even the Allante convertible failed to attract an audience, despite the prestige of being styled by Farina in Italy.

Cadillac fought back in the 1990s with their new Northstar engine, a V8 (what else?) that could run without coolant if required, and could go 100,000 miles without a service. In the event of coolant loss, the engine would revert to running

on fewer cylinders and use the air circulated by the non-firing pistons to cool the engine. The engine was mated to the biggest car that GM thought the public would buy, equipped with every modern gimmick they could devise, including computer-controlled suspension, ABS, variable-rate power-assisted steering, a computer-controlled stability system and traction control. With these designs Cadillac has come full circle, back to inspired designs using the finest technology available to it.

Chevrolet

Manufactured: 1911 to date.

The Name: The company was named after its founder, Louis Chevrolet.

The Badge: The Chevrolet badge is alleged to have been inspired by a design Chevrolet saw on the wallpaper in a Paris hotel.

History: Louis Chevrolet was born in Switzerland in 1878. He found early fame as a racing driver in Paris while working for Mors cars (where André Citroën would also work) before moving to Canada. From Canada he moved on to New York City, where he worked for the importers of French De Dion cars.

His ambitions led Louis Chevrolet to spend time with a number of car manufacturers, and in time he constructed a racing car to his own design based on Buick components. This car was mentioned to William Durant, founder of General Motors, by Louis's relation Arthur Chevrolet, who was his chauffeur at the time. Durant had lost control of General Motors by this time and was looking for new ways of making money.

Chevrolet and Durant jointly designed a new car for 1911 called the Classic Six. The Chevrolet name was chosen for the new range to cash in on the publicity arising from his racing fame. Production started at a factory in River Avenue, Detroit, and by November of 1911 the Chevrolet Motor Company was officially formed. There was a quick move across town to West Grand Boulevard as production grew faster than intended, and by 1912 nearly 3,000 cars had been sold.

Durant had previously been involved in the production of a small car called the Flint Buggy, and still had control of a number of small engineering concerns involved with that project. In 1913, production of the new Chevrolet moved again to Flint, where all Durant's companies were merged with the Chevrolet company. The Flint Buggy was renamed the 'Little Four' and continued in production alongside a number of derivatives.

Louis Chevrolet himself left the concern in 1913 to form the Chevrolet Aircraft Corporation and an engineering company, the Chevrolet Brothers Manufacturing Company. None of his companies weathered the Great Depression, and the man himself died in 1941.

Left: The re-styled Corvette of 1980 was the heir to a long sporting tradition in the Chevrolet stable.

Above right: In 1984 the potent ZR1 Corvette was a sports coupé for a whole new generation.

Below right: Even during the muddled years of the 1970s and early 1980s, the Corvette kept both its style and its popularity.

Behind the Wheel

The Chevrolet Company had purchased the Maxwell Car factory in 1914 as extra production space, and over 5,000 cars were assembled in that year alone. The following year saw the launch of the 490 model, so named because of its price, $490. In common with its rivals at Ford, Chevrolet had recognized the advantages of selling mass numbers to the economy sector of the market, and by 1916 it was selling over 70,000 vehicles a year. It branched out into commercial vehicles for the 1918 season and never looked back.

Chevrolet was taken over the General Motors in 1919, by which time production was close to 100,000 vehicles a year.

The post-First World War depression hit GM hard, with huge losses necessitating a swift reassessment of its objectives and model range. A damning outside report was taken as a challenge by the management, and by 1926 Chevrolet was the world's largest car manufacturer.

The successor to the successful 490 model was to have been the innovative air-cooled Superior, but major reliability problems led to a massive recall programme. Yet even in the face of such problems Chevrolet was opening plants all over the USA and produced over 200,000 cars per year. The magic 1 million cars per year was reached in 1927.

Having survived with a single basic four-cylinder engine design from the beginning, Chevrolet introduced a new six-cylinder design for 1929. Promoted as 'A six for the price of a four', it was another best-seller that allowed Chevrolet to weather the worldwide recession and remain America's best-selling car maker into the 1930s.

The early 1930s saw a range of improvements to the range. Synchromesh gearboxes allowing silent gearchanges, all-steel body shells, independent front suspension and hydraulic brakes were all standard fitments by 1936. The first Chevrolet Station Wagon was launched in 1939, and another styling icon had arrived.

The 10 millionth Chevrolet arrived in 1935, and the 15 millionth in 1939, before war work took over in 1941.

After a number of changes in directorship within GM, the Chevrolet range was totally restyled for the 1949 season. All the cars now wore sleek, low-slung bodies with plenty of chrome fittings. Big rear-wheel arches were the styling cue of the day.

The famous Bel Air coupé was launched in 1950, with even the cheapest models benefiting from automatic gearboxes. Yet another American motoring trend had been established. It was the

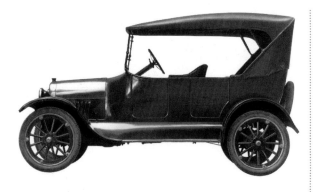

1954 season, however, that would see the arrival of the best known Chevrolet. Enter the Corvette.

Initially available as a two-seater convertible with a basic specification and an automatic gearbox, it was designed to beat the wave of imported British sports cars at their own game. Styled by Harvey J Earl, it featured a smoothly rounded body, a wrap-round windscreen and an understated chrome grille. Widely regarded as being underpowered in its initial form, it was fun to drive and was soon improved with the addition of a V8 engine and a manual gearbox for the 1955 season. The new Ford Thunderbird (which had been accused of having exactly the same faults as the Corvette when it was launched) now had a worthy rival.

1955 also saw the launch of the 'Tri-Chevys'. Although generally viewed as being the worst examples of over-the-top styling, they went on to find fame in hundreds of country music songs and videos. They offered everything the enthusiasts could want: saloons, Nomad station wagons, and big luxury convertibles with wide bench seats and vast rear fins. Despite only lasting three years (hence Tri-Chevys), their influence reached down the years and across all the other manufacturers' model ranges with their excessive fins and acres of chrome. Who can honestly say they have never heard of the 1957 Chevrolet?

In an attempt to get back to its roots Chevrolet launched the basic Corvair in 1959. Powered by a rear-mounted flat-six engine it was not well received by a motoring public more used to basic V8-engined saloons. There were also a number of well-publicized cases of handling problems which hit sales badly. Nevertheless, the Corvair soldiered on until 1969. At the same time as the launch of the Corvair, the more up-market models were renamed the Impala range, while the top of the line remained the Bel Air models.

The sleek coupé version of the old Corvette, the Stingray, also arrived in 1962. Now sporting a 5.7-litre V8 it offered very rapid performance for its price. A Camaro coupé joined the range in 1969 as a competitor to the Ford Mustang.

Under the auspices of GM, Chevrolet engines were now being fitted to many other models within the range. The larger of the German Opels gained the V8s, while the smaller Oldsmobiles used the smaller six-cylinder engines. Specialist small-scale manufacturers in Europe also found the compact V8s useful, buyers including Gordon Keeble of England and ISO of Italy.

The worldwide fuel crisis of the early 1970s led to a rapid downsizing of the Chevrolet range, with the recently purchased Isuzu being used as a source of ideas and technology. 1971 saw the arrival of the small Vega, and it was joined by GM's 'world car', the Chevette, in 1976.

Despite a diverse and interesting range of cars, Chevrolet lost its number-one spot in the car-making galaxy in 1980; by 1990 it was actually making massive losses in the region of $800 million a month. A swift reorganization followed, with many established models being dropped

and production methods being streamlined. In 1992 Chevrolet offered no less than thirty-eight different cars and eighty different commercial vehicles spread over twenty-one different floorpans. A grand plan was announced to reduce this number to seven basic floorpans and to increase vastly the interchangeability of parts within the ranges.

With the new century Chevrolet is starting to show signs of fresh vigour, with new models being announced and its market share rising again. How long before it is number one once more?

Facing page, above: The early Chevrolets, like this 1920 model, were designed as popular, sensibly priced transport for the masses.

Facing page, below: The first car to wear the Corvette name was a simple design with a fibreglass body and an automatic gearbox, intended to combat cheap British sports car imports at their own game.

Above left: Chevrolet's publicity shots of its 1963 Corvair 500 Coupé. The rear-engined Corvair quickly gained a reputation for poor handling, and the model was dropped in 1969 after ten years in production.

Above right: The Corvette Sting Ray – this is a 1963 convertible – is considered by many to be the ultimate Corvette.

Right: The early Corvette – like this 1954 model – could be had with a handsome hard top for all-weather motoring in wetter climates.

Citroën

Manufactured: 1919 to date.

The Name: The make was named after its founder, André Citroën.

The Badge: The double-chevron badge was adopted as a symbol of the revolutionary double-helical gears Citroën was famous for designing.

History: André Citroën graduated from the famous École Polytechnique of Paris in 1908 and set up in business producing the helical gears he adopted as his company symbol. His expertise in engineering saw him appointed technical director at the Mors car company. While there he redesigned their production facilities for greater efficiency before starting out on his own in 1913.

During the First World War, the French government helped Citroën to purchase a large factory in Paris where he could put his genius for manufacturing methods into producing munitions for the war effort. Through the use of hi-tech American tools and methods he became one of the most efficient producers of shells in the world. After the war Citroën decided to dedicate his factory to the production of low-budget motor cars after visiting America to examine their advanced production methods.

His first production design was (logically) the Model A, a cheap, mass-produced vehicle in the mould of the Ford Model T. With his modern production-line system, Citroën could produce more of his cars at a cheaper rate than any of his competitors, and sales reflected this.

A bigger-engined Type B followed in 1921, closely followed by a Type C, intended to appeal to women drivers. This was dropped in 1926 when Citroën realized that he could make more money by concentrating on his larger cars.

Already branching out, Citroën produced commercial vehicles from 1923, and set up his own taxi company which exclusively used Citroën vehicles. For 1932 he founded the Société des Transports André Citroën, which was a coach company that offered services to all corners of France. Once again, it made full and exclusive use of Citroën vehicles.

Citroën was an early advocate of advertising and one of the first car makers to advertise in national newspapers. He also had his name up in lights on the Eiffel Tower, as well as sky-written in the air above Paris. He even posted gramo-

phone records to prospective customers to tell them about his products.

His name was seldom out of the newsreels, as his half-tracks were the vehicles regularly chosen by expeditions to every obscure corner of the world, and wherever expeditions went, they always took a camera to record the events. A Citroën B2 half-track was the first car to cross the Sahara, and C4 models would be driven across Central Asia and the arctic regions of Canada.

Citroën adopted pressed-steel car bodies after the American practice in 1924, enabling him to improve the production-line methods he had championed from the beginning. The B series was the first to benefit from these new bodies, and next the Type C range was launched with a mixture of four- and six-cylinder engines for 1928. When the Type C range was replaced by the Rosalie range of 1932 Citroën actively sought coachbuilders who would be prepared to build

custom bodies and interiors for his mass-produced body shells and chassis. With their help he was able to list more than eighty different models in his catalogue.

The car that would make Citroën famous arrived in 1934, when the whole range of Rosalie models was replaced by the revolutionary Traction Avant models. Literally translated as 'front traction' this was the first mass-produced front-wheel-drive car. In place of the classic chassis/bolt-on body system was a fully welded monocoque structure. In this form the car's body is made up of welded and fully stressed structures such as sills and box sections to give it strength and rigidity. The engine was mounted on a separate subframe like the Mini of the 1960s, and the suspension was an advanced fully independent torsion-bar system. The engine was an all-new unit, and the body was styled with a sleek sloping radiator grille that could not be confused with any other car's.

The car lasted until 1967, but the costs of getting it into production forced Citroën into bankruptcy. The concern was taken over by Michelin in 1934, and André Citroën himself died in 1935.

After the Second World War, Citroën looked towards the mass market for its next product. A design specification was set that stated the new car had to be able to transport two farmers in comfort across a ploughed field without breaking the

Facing page, below: Citroën's Traction Avant model made front-wheel drive fashionable all over Europe and led to some rapid redesigning on the part of the other car manufacturers. This example is from the 1940s, but the car was in production from 1934 to 1967.

Above: The innovative and idiosyncratic Citroën GS was voted European Car of the Year in 1971.

Right: Perhaps the most famous Citroën of all, the futuristic and equally innovative DS, introduced in 1955, offered a true floating-on-air ride via hydraulic suspension at a time when many other manufacturers were still using cart springs.

43

contents of a basket of eggs. There were also stipulations about the vehicle's economy and simplicity, and the result was the Deux Chevaux (2-horsepower) or 2CV.

Returning to the older chassis/bolt-on body building style, the 2CV featured a flat-twin engine and a roll-back plastic roof, rather than a metal panel, to keep weight down. Despite its total lack of performance and the incredible amount of body roll apparent on even the slightest corner, the 2CV became an instant cult car. Christened the 'Tin Snail' by its detractors, production finished in 1988 in France, and continued afterwards in plants in Portugal. Some enthusiasts even race them in their own special series. In time the range was joined by more powerful versions called the Ami and the Dyane, but neither survived the 1970s.

The larger Citroën models were replaced in 1955 in the form of the DS (or Goddess, since French *déesse*, the phonetic pronunciation of the initials, means just that). This was a revolution in comfort and style. Pioneering a clever system of a structural skeleton similar to the Superleggera system, the entire outer body shell was made up of unstressed panels easily replaced in the event of an accident.

Every conceivable gadget was present, and everything was hydraulically powered. There was hydraulic self-levelling suspension to give a remarkably smooth ride, power steering and a futuristic interior that could have been inspired

by a pulp-magazine spaceship. Later versions featured auxiliary driving lights that followed the direction of the steering wheel, and there was even fuel injection for the 1969 season.

For 1970 there was a brief flirtation with exotica in the form of the SM. This was a modified big Citroën with a Maserati engine that lasted until 1975. Usually built to special order only, they are a rare sight today.

The mid-sized GS saloon joined the range in 1971 and made use of the family hydraulic system and an air-cooled flat-four engine which bucked the trend of every other manufacturer in Europe. It was voted European Car of the Year for 1971 for its innovative design and excellent ride.

The big DS range was replaced by the more conventionally styled CS for 1974, but under the smooth skin the usual Citroën idiosyncrasies remained. Everything was powered, and the hydraulic suspension lived on unchanged. It was great when it worked, but once neglected by later owners, it could become an expensive curse.

Peugeot purchased Citroën in 1975, and the next new Citroën was the small LNA. It was created by basically fitting the Citroën flat-twin engine to the Peugeot 104, and later small Citroëns even made use of Peugeot engines.

The glory days of Citroën innovation have passed.

Is That Really True?

The Traction Avant Citroën will always be known as the 'Maigret Citroën' in England, after its extensive use in the 1960s TV show *Maigret* by the star Rupert Davies.

For a brief period Citroën UK built a 2CV derivative called the Bijou. Using the normal 2CV chassis and mechanics it featured a heavier fibreglass body shell and was even slower than the French original. It lasted from 1959-1964, and only around 200 were produced.

Daimler

Manufactured: 1896 to date.

The Name: Daimler was originally founded as the British arm of the German company of the same name, which was in turn named after its founder, Gottlieb Daimler.

The Badge: Daimlers were badged with a simple Daimler script with a large flourish to the initial D. Some models wore a flying 'D' mascot.

History: Daimler is one of the few companies that can truly say it was around at the beginning of motoring; a Daimler was the first car to complete the Land's End to John-o'-Groats journey in 1897.

These first cars were better described as 'horseless carriages', simple open designs that looked as if they only needed shafts to be pulled along by horses. Even windscreens had yet to arrive as coach drivers were not felt to need such things.

The company's first products were simple twin-cylinder designs, but the high-speed development of the time meant they had over forty different models listed before the coming of the First World War and a change to munitions production. They also had interests in boat and commercial-vehicle production.

The smaller twin-cylinder models took a back seat from 1909, when larger four- and six-cylinder cars with chain drive started to appear. Always plush and luxurious, big engines meant that even the heaviest of these early Daimlers were sprightly performers by the standards of the day. Nevertheless, they soon became better known for being big, quiet cars rather than sporting machines.

For the 1909/1910 season Daimler changed its engine designs to make use of the new sleeve-valve technology produced by the Knight group. Using this system the Daimler range restarted

Right: A British car with a German name – this wartime Daimler advertisement manages to appeal to patriotism, admiration for technical brilliance, and the traditions of the Royal Navy.

car production after the war and quietly continued selling its wares to well-off customers for whom only the best would do.

The first V12-engined Daimler arrived in 1927, and would remain in production in one size or another until 1938. Engine sizes varied from as small as 1.9 litres up to a mighty 7.1. These made the cars as fast and quiet as any other on the road, confidently able to stand alongside the likes of Rolls-Royce and Bentley.

Daimler purchased the Lanchester marque in 1931 and used it as a smaller luxury make slightly down market from its ever larger cars. In time Lanchester would fall into badge engineering, and the name would be allowed to pass into history in 1956.

The engine range was lightly updated for 1933, and 1935 saw the adoption of a straight-eight engine that was used in a number of cars. Most notable of these was the Light Straight Eight, a sporty convertible, complete with

Men who design finer and faster machines choose this car for their own use

Daimler

exposed exhaust pipes emerging from the side of the bonnet and a long sloping tail, that closely mirrored American tastes of the time.

The vast and diverse range of cars available continued in stately fashion until the Second World War brought things to a halt again. As car production ended Daimler was still offering a huge range of bodies, styles and engine sizes to suit just about any of its up-market customers.

Production restarted in 1946 in the usual manner. Pre-war designs were reintroduced after a mild makeover and occasional renaming.

The pre-war DB18 cars were available as saloons, limousines or sports tourers. All were fitted with a straight-six engine of 2.5 litres that would soldier on until 1953. The more well-off customers were taken care of by the DE27, a 4.1-litre straight-eight that came as a limousine, luxury saloon and (curiously) ambulance. Those with even more money to play with could order the last straight-eight to remain in production in the UK, the mighty DE36 with a 5.4-litre engine.

The DE36 would go on to be used in the first of the 'Docker specials' of the 1950s. By this time the Daimler empire had been taken over by the wealthy Docker family, of whom the most extravagant was Lady Docker.

Somewhat of a media figure of the day, she commissioned a number of outrageous Daimler specials for the 1952–5 Motor Shows. These featured such excesses as gold-plated brightwork and zebra-skin upholstery. If publicity for the Daimler name was the aim, they succeeded beyond her wildest dreams, but the sheer costs involved eventually led to a management revolt which saw the Dockers deposed as controllers of the Daimler company.

A whole new straight-six-engined range was launched for 1953/1954. Given such stirring and patriotic names as Regency, Conquest and Empress, they were more in a sporting style than the cars that had gone before, and brought up-to-date styling to what had become a dated range. All were offered with the usual Daimler range of body styles, and there was even a sporting

Is That Really True?

Early motoring enthusiast King Edward VII used Daimlers from 1900, and the English royal family continued to use Daimlers into the 1950s, when they adopted other makes.

Not content with marketing a vast range of luxury cars, Daimler produced buses from 1908, and during the 1920s and 1930s they produced small cars under the BSA name.

The Daimler Conquest of 1953 was so named because it was priced at £1066, the date of the Norman invasion of England.

When Jaguar purchased the Daimler company, it briefly considered using the 4.5-litre Majestic Major engine in a Daimler-badged version of the large MkX saloons. The prototype proved to be embarrassingly faster than Jaguar's own version, and the plans were quietly dropped.

Right: The interior of the Jaguar-based Daimlers, like this 1977 Double-Six Vanden Plas, was derived from their parent cars. Daimler examples almost always had full leather upholstery and even more luxurious fittings than the Jaguars.

Below: The Jaguar XJ6-based Daimlers were every bit as fast and comfortable as what had gone before. Only their individuality was a casualty of the merger, as this shot of a 1977 Double-Six Vanden Plas shows.

Conquest roadster, the first sports Daimler since before the war. The limousine market aimed at royalty had a last flowering in the Regina, desperately trying to regain the Royal Warrant the company was losing to Rolls-Royce.

1959 saw the arrival of the Edward Turner-designed V8 range. Having already designed the famous Triumph Speed Twin motorcycle engine he delivered to Daimler one of the finest and most flexible engines ever designed. Available in 2.5- and 4.5-litre forms, they went on to power the entire Daimler range. The big 4.5-litre version went into the Majestic Major and DR450 to make some of the fastest hearses and limousines of their day. Despite their heavy coachwork, both displayed excellent handling that belied their sheer size.

Also for 1959 Daimler made a surprise announcement of a new sports car. Initially named the Dart, it was hastily renamed the SP250 for production after complaints from American truck manufacturer Dodge, who had the rights to the name.

With its then revolutionary fibreglass body the SP250 was reported to be able to go 'from 5 to 125mph in top gear', such was the flexibility of the Turner-designed engine. With a curvy body that was politely described as controversial by the motoring press, it was not to everyone's taste, but it sold well by Daimler's standards. Worries about the stiffness of the chassis were raised when doors were found likely to open themselves during spirited cornering. This was quickly addressed by updates to the basic design.

Jaguar took control of Daimler in 1960, and the first product of the liaison was the SP250 saloon. A mating of the Turner 2.5-litre V8 with the small Jaguar MkII body shell, it produced a sporting drive, and Daimler enthusiasts argue that it is a better car than the original Jaguar.

The SP250 sports car was dropped in 1964 to stop competition with Jaguar's own E-Type range, and the saloon was put to rest in 1969 when production of the Jaguar equivalent ceased. From now on the Daimler name would only live on in badge-engineered versions of Jaguar saloons, and a sole limousine based on the Jaguar 420G floorpan and powered by the Jaguar XK engine.

Ferrari

Manufactured: 1938 to date.

The Name: The company was named after its founder, Enzo Ferrari.

The Badge: While driving for Alfa Romeo, Ferrari won a number of races at the Savio circuit for which he was congratulated by Count Baracca, son of the First World War fighter ace Francesco Baracca. The pilot had been killed in 1918, and his widow gave Ferrari permission to use his prancing-horse emblem on his cars.

History: Enzo Ferrari was born in 1898 in Modena, Italy, and had learned to drive the family car by the time he was thirteen. The family business lay in the manufacture of railway equipment, which Ferrari worked in until both his brother and father died in 1916.

Ferrari enlisted in the Italian army in 1917, eventually getting the chance to practise his mechanical skills by working with aero engines. Invalided out of the service in 1918, he used his contacts to get car-testing work, which led to his first competitive drive in a hill climb in 1919. For his 'proper' job, he worked for an engineering company in Bologna that rebodied army-surplus trucks into family saloons and sports cars. Ferrari eventually ended up working for Alfa Romeo as one of their racing drivers, and it was while there that he encountered Paolina, Countess Baracca, who would dedicate her late husband's prancing-horse emblem to his cars.

Ferrari retired from active racing driving when his son, Dino, was born in 1932. By this time he had already left Alfa Romeo to form his own company, Societa Anonima Scuderia Ferrari. He and his colleagues were involved with the designing, modifying and racing of other people's cars. Alfa Romeos featured heavily in their activities, despite its having fallen into state ownership in 1932 in the face of mounting debts.

He found himself back with Alfa Romeo proper in 1938 with the formation of Alfa Corse, the company's official racing team. This time he was there as manager, but he left within a year after disputes with the engineering staff. Using the severance pay from Alfa Romeo, and the remaining capital from his earlier concern, Ferrari was able to form his own engineering company. Starting out as a tool manufacturer, he soon started to design cars, even though he was not permitted to use his own name on them as one of the conditions of his parting with Alfa Romeo.

Ferrari's first car, which was briefly produced between late 1939 and mid-1940, was the Tipo 815. Powered by a straight-eight engine, it featured a body by Touring coachbuilders of Milan and a selection of Fiat parts.

As with most car manufacturers, Ferrari production was halted for the duration of the Second World War, and when it restarted Enzo announced

Left: The 1956 Ferrari 410 Superamerica. This, the first of the Superamerica range, sported an engine of nearly 5 litres and suitably fashionable tail fins.

Right: The 250GTO is widely regarded as being the ultimate road-going racing car from the Ferrari stable.

that from now on he would be using his own name on his cars. That first car was a V12 1.5-litre called the 125, quickly followed by two larger-engined models, the 159 and the 166. The latter would go on to become the first truly road-going Ferrari, the 166 Inter; both were sleek coupés with long-nosed bodies built over a space-frame chassis.

A link was made with famous American racing driver Briggs Cunningham, and the first Ferrari arrived in the USA in 1949. American demands for bigger engines led to the 400 and 410 Superamerica models, eventually leading to the 4.9-litre Superfast with an engine output of 400 bhp. These were aimed purely at the American market, and their styling made them look a little like the contemporary Ford Thunderbird, with overtones of the Corvette from some angles.

The Superfast was to be the last of the relatively crude, front-engined coupés aimed at the American market, however. From 1966 the Americans were supplied with European-style cars altered just enough to be able to pass the ever more stringent American emissions and safety laws.

Ferrari cars continued to have successes in racing, taking their first Grand Prix win in Britain and winning the Mille Miglia in 1951. They would go on to take nine world championships and nine wins at the Le Mans 24-hour race. When Ford decided it wanted a win at Le Mans in the 1960s, it tried to buy Ferrari, but Enzo would not hand over control of his racing programme and stayed stubbornly independent. Instead he continued to support the Lancia team, as he had from 1955.

1954 saw the arrival of the Ferrari 250, a long-distance GT that was ideal for touring the fast-growing network of European motorways. This was joined in 1961 by his first car with four seats in the form of the 250 two-plus-two. Lightweight competition versions naturally followed, but were only built in tiny numbers.

Ferrari rewrote the rulebook in America in 1968 with the introduction of the Daytona, named to commemorate Ferrari's success at the 24-hour race of the same name. Still with the mighty Ferrari V12 in the front, it was sharply-styled and could boast a top speed of 175mph. It would last until 1974, and is still highly valued by collectors today.

In memory of his recently deceased son, Ferrari designed a small V6-engined sports coupé that would bear the Dino rather than the Ferrari

Above: Ferrari road cars have always played seconnd fiddle to their larger racing brothers, like this 1967 330.

Left: The Ferrari Daytona – this is a 365 GT/4 – featured the famous V12 engine mounted at the front to give a long-nosed car with excellent dynamics.

Right: The original Testa Rossa (literally, red head) was a racing Ferrari so called after its red-painted cylinder heads. Pictured here is a 250 Testa Rossa of the 1950s.

badge. As with so many Ferraris, larger engines quickly followed the initial 2-litre unit, and the basic style lasted until 1974.

Fiat took a controlling interest in Ferrari in 1969, and would go on to take over most of the Italian motor industry during the 1970s and 1980s. True to its usual form it continued to allow Ferrari to build the sort of cars he had been famous for, and most people did not even realize that the company that produced the tiny 126 was also responsible for some of the world's fastest cars.

The well-known V12 was changed for the Grand Prix-inspired 365GTBB Berlinetta Boxer. Now it was replaced by a flat-twelve engine mounted in the middle of the car for better weight distribution. Again showing sharp, up-to-the-minute styling, the car would go on to give birth to that modern legend, the Testarossa (red head), capable of 180mph. Its deeply cut side air intakes make it as instantly identifiable on the road as the swing-up doors of its Lamborghini competitor.

For 1987 Enzo Ferrari produced what is regarded by many as his finest creation: the F40, launched and named to commemorate the company's forty years in the business. The last car to be overseen by the man himself before he died in 1989, it was the fastest road car available at the time. Capable of out-accelerating just about any other production car, it would go on to a frightening maximum speed of 201mph. Yet it was surpassed by the F50 of 1997 which sported a V12 engine over the original's turbocharged V8. By now the Jaguar XJ220 and Lamborghini Diablo had arrived, and the world's-fastest-car title was under heavy competition. All these machines could top 200mph with ease, and for most drivers surely that has to be enough?

Fiat

Manufactured: 1899 to date.

The Name: F.I.A.T. stands for Fabbrica Italiana di Automobili Torino.

The Badge: The badge is the company's name in simple type, frequently surrounded by a winner's garland to commemorate their early racing victories.

History: The company was founded by nine entrepreneurs from Piedmont on 1 July, 1899. Chief among them were Giovanni Agnelli and Count Carlo Biscaretti di Ruffia.

Their first car was a rear-engined buggy in the horseless-carriage style, providing very basic seating for two people, protected by an open-fronted hood that could be raised or lowered. By 1901 the engine had been moved to the front and uprated, although the body style remained largely the same.

Cars that today's driver would recognize arrived in 1902, powered by a 3.7-litre four-cylinder engine. Still largely open to the elements, these Fiats were joined by the even larger 10-litre car for 1905. The smaller runabouts were quietly discontinued as the four-cylinder models started to take precedence.

An engine of 11 litres arrived for 1907, and shaft drive took over from earlier chains in the same year. With these massive engines and an outlook open to modern technology, Fiat soon found success in racing. Overhead camshafts and overhead valves, at a time when sleeve- and side-valve engines were the more usual fare, raised a few eyebrows among the competition, but the cars kept on winning. The engine-size race came to a halt with the might 26-litre, 130mph Fiat racer of 1910. Given the technology of the day, it must have been a frightening car to drive, or, more worryingly, to try to stop.

By the outbreak of the First World War, Fiat was producing a wide range of cars for all sections of the market. The most successful was the compact Type Zero, so named because it was smaller than the earlier Type 1.

After the war, Fiat introduced a range of more streamlined designs, having produced over 35,000 vehicles for the war effort. The first car launched, and the first mass-produced Fiat, was the Type (Tipo) 501. A small, practical car with a 1.5-litre engine, it was aimed at the market later occupied by the Austin Seven and Morris Minor of a few years later. It was available in a range of body styles, and soon gained a reputation for reliability.

The early 1920s were marked by the introduction of a range of Superfiats, powered by a new 6.8-litre V12 engine. All were big touring cars in the Daimler and Bentley mould, and most still came with open compartments for the driver to sit in, while the rear was enclosed.

In 1925 the new small Fiat, the 509, was launched. Powered by an advanced 990cc engine it offered sprightly performance at an affordable price. It was closely followed by the equally well-liked if slightly larger 508 Balilla model of 1932

Left: The first Fiats were truly horseless carriages, as this picture of Fiat No. 1 in 1899 shows.

Above right: An original Fiat advertisement from 1899, the year the company was founded.

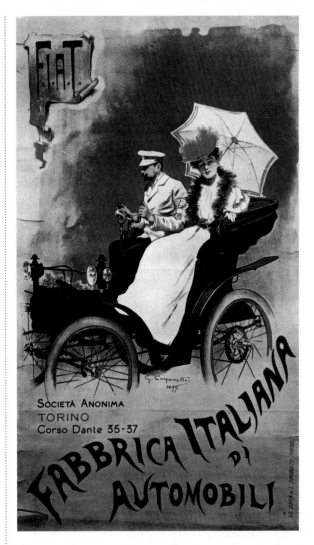

The 508 would go on to be a popular competition car and would be made under licence in both Poland and France.

The car that made Fiat famous was launched in 1936, the Topolino, or Mouse. Featuring a small 570cc engine it could carry two people in comfort, if not silence, anywhere there was a road. It was the first of a line of small Fiats that would make the company famous all over the world.

After the war, Fiat hurried its little Topolino, now known as the 500 or Cinquecento, back into production. Ideally priced for a struggling Italian economy desperate for transport, it continued its pre-war success.

Fiat also produced a wide range of 1100/1500 saloons and estates, though they were seldom seen outside of Italy. There was even a V8-engined sports coupé for 1952, but poor sales led to it being abandoned after two seasons. It was for small cars that Italy would continue to be known.

The 500 was replaced by the 600 for 1955, and there was even a six-seater people-carrier with a slightly larger engine. Abarth produced tuned versions, and a plant in Argentina continued to produce them well into the 1980s, by when Fiat had long since moved on.

The tiny 500 was back for 1957, complete with a howling rear-mounted, air-cooled twin-cylinder engine that struggled to push the car along at any-thing like the speed limit. But compared with the likes of the Citroën 2CV it all made a strange sort of sense. There were 'Jolly' convertibles by Vignale, and even a tiny estate car called the Giardiniera (Gardener).

At the time when Fiat was making a name for itself with its tiny transports, its big saloons were starting to feature advanced six-cylinder engines and the early forebears of the twin-cam unit that would consolidate the company's reputation in the 1970s.

The rear-engined family was increased for 1965 with the arrival of the 850. A full-sized car with the engine at the back, it handled superbly, and even gave rise to a sporty coupé and a small convertible aimed at the MG Midget market.

The family market was served by the square 124/125 range from the mid-1960s, which would go on to be used as a pattern for local cars all over the world when Fiat finished with them in 1972 (see panel, p. 53). Some featured that famous twin-cam engine, although popular belief has it that their handling was not up to the extra power.

An exception was the 124 Spider. A generous convertible in the Triumph Stag style, it lasted for twenty years before Fiat could no longer keep up with American regulations and allowed it to fade in 1985.

The faithful 500 was finally replaced by the almost equally tiny 126 in 1977, and the family range was replaced by the compact 127 and the Strada models. Both the latter became best-sellers, and offered particularly good value for money as well as generous equipment levels.

Slotted somewhere in the range was an abnormality that arrived in 1978. The Italian coachbuilder Bertone took a Strada floorpan and fitted a Fiat engine across the middle to create the handsome X 1/9 sports car. Featuring impeccable handling, sharp styling and a lift-off roof it was a quiet sales success that no one expected, lasting until 1989. Selling alongside it was the ultra-basic Panda model, a square utility vehicle with no aspirations to be anything other than basic transport in the Topolino mould – it would go on to become one of Fiat's success stories following a government drive to scrap old vehicles in the late 1990s. The Panda was sold at a bargain price to keep people moving when they scrapped their old cars, and when the scrap drive was over the car just kept on selling.

The Uno small hatchback went on sale in 1983 to become one of Europe's best-selling cars, and its replacement, the Punto, looks set to do the same again. Yet as history has shown many times, Fiat just cannot seem to do well with its large cars. Everyone remembers the 500, the 127, the Panda, and even the little 126. But who can picture the 132 saloon, even though it was a quick, reliable car of it's day? Nevertheless, with its ownership, among others of Ferrari, Lancia, Alfa Romeo, Fiat remains one of the world's greatest car makers.

Ford (USA)

Manufactured: 1901 to date.
The Name: The cars were named after the company's founder, Henry Ford.
The Badge: The cars are badged with Ford's name in script.
History: Henry Ford completed his first car in 1896. This was not a car as the modern motorist would know it, but a 'quadricycle', essentially a four-wheeled bicycle built to accommodate two-abreast seating with an engine and crude rudder-style steering. This and a second vehicle built in 1899 impressed his backers, the Detroit Automobile Company, to the extent that they put the designs into production.

Poor sales and a character clash led Henry Ford to leave the company and turn his interests to motor racing. A win in a car of his own design at the 1901 Grosse Point race track in Detroit led to further funding, which in turn led to him being able to found the Henry Ford Company in November 1901. Ford's interests remained in racing, however, and in February 1902 he left with a settlement of $900 and an agreement that

Below: The Model A roadster of the 1920s and 30s featured a body style popular among Ford buyers.

the company would change its name. It did so – to Cadillac – and the rest is history.

During 1902 Ford built a pair of 8hp racing cars named 'Arrow' and '999'. Despite the cars being hard to drive, professional racing driver Barney Oldfield won the 1902 Manufacturer's Challenge Cup by covering a five-mile course in five minutes twenty-eight seconds. This attracted plenty of publicity to Ford, and in June 1903 the Ford Motor Company was formed.

Above left: The original Ford product, the Quadricyle of 1896. Henry Ford had to demolish part of his workshop to get the finished vehicle out.

Above: A 1909 advertisement for Ford's Model T, launched the year before.

Below left: Advertisement for the Model T's predecessors in 1905 – the Models B and C.

The first car was called the Model A. A light 8hp model, it sold well and was quickly followed by the other letters of the alphabet until the Model K was reached in 1903. This was Ford's first six-cylinder car, and it was his first sales flop. There was not yet a market in America for big cars, whereas in Europe almost all the major manufacturers had started out with big cars and moved down-market as sales required. Even so, by 1906 Ford was selling nearly 15,000 cars a year.

The year 1908 was a milestone in the world of motoring. Ford introduced the Model T, affectionately known as the 'Tin Lizzie' – the cheap, basic car that put America on wheels. When Ford introduced the world's first production line in 1914, prices tumbled. A basic Model T of 1911 cost $950, but by 1925 it cost a mere $290. The Highland Park factory in Detroit was the largest in the world at the time, and there Ford pioneered the concept of the moving production line which enabled his factories to build cars faster than any other company of the time. The modern concept of the car factory had arrived.

Model T sales had started to fall by the middle of the 1920s, however. Henry Ford refused to admit that his design was anything but perfect, believing he would be able to keep making them for ever, but customers were starting to demand more comfort and refinement for their money, and in 1927 Model T production finally ceased. It was replaced by a new Model A late in 1927, which was another instant sales success.

In 1932, with the Great Depression at its height, Ford gambled on public tastes and produced his first budget V8. The side-valve engine was a simple but sturdy design, and went on to become the mainstay of Ford production until it was replaced in 1953. The smaller four-cylinder engines were dropped in 1933.

The 1930s were great days for Ford, even though it lost the number-one sales position in America to Chevrolet. But Henry Ford's dedication to certain outdated practices (such as mechanical rather than hydraulic brakes), as well as his open admiration of certain discredited political factions in Europe, did much to undermine his public image. His harsh resistance to the

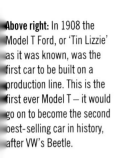

Above right: In 1908 the Model T Ford, or 'Tin Lizzie' as it was known, was the first car to be built on a production line. This is the first ever Model T – it would go on to become the second best-selling car in history, after VW's Beetle.

Right: The Model A saloon was a best-seller for Ford in the 1930s. Shown here is a 'two-window, four-door' model of 1932.

Left: A 1957 Ford Thunderbird. The 'T-bird' was large, underpowered and had soft handling, but even so, Ford were able to sell as many as they could make.

Facing page, below: The Ford Mustang was responsible for the naming of the 'Pony Car' concept of fitting the largest engine possible into a basic saloon car.

coming of unions in his factories also did little to endear him to the American working man.

While its cars continued to sell well through the 1940s, Ford was undergoing an unhappy time. Henry Ford's son Edsel died suddenly in 1943, and a power struggle began within the company for the post of vice-president. The US Govern-

---

Is That Really True?

The Ford Thunderbird was named after a magical symbol used by the Pueblo Indians.

For 1957 and 1958, Ford produced a truly unique car, the Fairlane Skyliner. Outwardly a typical if rather large saloon of the period, it featured a retractable metal coupé top. At the touch of a button the metal hardtop lifted off, moved backwards and stowed out of sight in the boot.

Henry Ford was the man who, in 1914, introduced the world to the concept of the eight-hour working day.

Ford was also famous for saying of his Model T, 'You can have any colour you like as long as it's black'.

---

ment became concerned about the potential problems at Ford as they relied on it for large amounts of mechanical war material. They therefore arranged for Henry Ford II, the eldest of Edsel's children, to leave the US Navy and assume the position of vice-president. The original Henry Ford, now over eighty years old, retired in 1945, and died two years later.

In the aftermath of the Second World War, Ford found itself in trouble. With its lucrative war-materials contracts at an end, and only an outdated range of cars to sell, losses soared. Thankfully its first new models, the Tudor range, were a sales success. An up-to-date vehicle powered by the Ford V8 engine and smoothly styled in the fashion of the time, it was the right product at the right time.

By the early 1950s Henry Ford II was set on overtaking Chevrolet and putting Ford back in the number-one sales spot. His range of cars included the basic Fords, the more up-market Edsels, the luxury sporting Mercurys and the Continental range, the latter designed to knock wheels with the likes of Cadillac and Packard.

Unable to meet the cost-cutting and economies of scale available to the giants like

Behind the Whee

Ford, the 1950s saw the demise of many of the great names in American motoring.

To meet the flood of British sports cars into America and Chevrolet's newly launched Corvette range, Ford launched the Thunderbird in 1955. Despite having a trendy modern-styled body, underneath it was powered by basic saloon-car mechanics, exactly the same system as British manufacturers were using to produce their cheap sports cars. What it lacked in performance and handling, however, it more than made up for in comfort, looks and presence. A big car by European standards, it was ideal for the American looking for his first 'fun' car, and Ford couldn't make them fast enough.

1960 saw the arrival of Lee Iacocca at Ford. He was the force behind the Ford 'Total Performance' marketing strategy and the Mustang project. The idea behind this was simple. Take a basic car, make it available in saloon, coupé and convertible form, then drop in the largest engine you can find to give it blistering performance. The first of the breed, the Mustang, gave its name to the whole concept. The 'Pony Car' had been born. With a wide range of engines available, the most famous of the Mustangs was the potent Boss model. Powered by a 7-litre engine, it was an instant winner on race circuits everywhere and a sales success until the fuel crisis of the 1970s started to take hold.

The 1970s were rough years for the whole American car industry, and Ford was no exception. With fuel prices rising, its previous reliance on large cars with big engines made it unpopular with the buying public. For the first time smaller Japanese cars started to make inroads in the American market.

Like most other American manufacturers, Ford radically downsized its ranges. The mighty Mustang and Thunderbird models became mere shadows of their former selves, and the 'world car' concept was born. Put simply, new designs were built to appeal to markets all over the world, rather than just to their domestic markets. By the 1980s, Fords emerging from plants all over the world looked very much the same. Mazda engines were used in some of the smaller models, and even the Japanese motorcycle manufacturer Yamaha was employed to develop a new range of light, efficient engines. The days when Ford UK, Ford USA and Ford Germany all produced different models were gone. And since profits soared, from a corporate standpoint at least, downsizing must have been the right decision.

Ford (UK)

Manufactured: 1911 to date.

History: In the UK, Ford cars, including the famous Model T, were assembled at a plant in Trafford Park, Manchester from 1911 before moving to a vast new factory at Dagenham in 1931. With this new plant it now had the space to develop and produce cars of its own design, for the big, lazy cars designed for the American markets were far from suitable for smaller British roads.

The first product was the Model Y 8hp. A small, basic car with rounded styling and a simple side-valve engine, its price had fallen to £100 by 1935. This made it the first full-sized car on the British market to be offered for such a low sum, and a larger 10hp model joined the range in the same year.

A V8 modelled on the American parent company's products was scaled down and produced as the 22hp, and before the Second World War

Above: For the 1951 Earls Court Motor Show, Ford's advertisement features the company's entire range of cars

Left: Until the VW Beetle overtook it, Ford's Model T – or 'Tin Lizzie' – was the world's best-selling car, and was produced from 1908 to 1927. This advertisement shows a right-hand-drive model.

THE *Ford* TIMES

halted most production, the well-known Anglia Popular and Prefect names had their first outings on derivatives of 8/10hp models.

Production of the Prefect van continued during the war, but the rest of the range was given a compulsory rest until 1945. They were then al reintroduced with few, if any, changes, and would

run largely unchanged until they were finally laid to rest in 1959. The Popular had continued to be the cheapest car in the in the UK for most of this time, but by the time production ceased its day had long passed. The big Ford V8s of pre-war years were briefly reawakened as the handsome Pilot range, but were abandoned in 1950.

Other parts of the Ford range had moved up-market with the handsome and well remembered Consul/Zephyr/Zodiac range. Big, soft saloons (there was a convertible option) with a lazy column gearchange, they were clearly influenced by their American brethren. The up-market models were covered with chrome in the fashion of the time and soon found fame as the 'Teddy Boy' cars of the era. The revolutionary Macpherson strut

independent suspension made its debut with this model, and was to remain a trademark of the Ford range.

The small-car range was replaced at the 1953 Earl's Court Motor Show with the new Anglia/Prefect range. With updated versions of the old side-valve engine, they now had monococque bodies as opposed to the old-style separate-chassis construction, and they too used the new suspension system.

Above left: The Ford Zephyr 6 of 1954. Note the Royal Warrant at top left.

Above right: The Ford Squire estate car as advertised in 1958.

Right: Ford UK's Escort of the 1980s, like this 1987 GL, was the fourth generation to wear that badge with pride. It sold in millions the world over.

For reasons best known to Ford, the old-style engine-vacuum-driven windscreen wipers were retained, as was the three-speed gearbox, when most of the opposition offered electric wipers and four speeds. The result was wipers that slowed down and sometime even stopped when the car was labouring up a steep hill, and a gearbox that has been unkindly described as just having third gear taken out.

On the styling front, however, their neat, square shape still looked fresh when they were replaced for the 1959 season by a new Anglia. This one had a new overhead-valve engine, a proper four-speed gearbox and electric wipers. Perhaps best remembered for the styling cue of a rear window that sloped inwards from top to bottom, it was perfectly shaped to make use of the fashion for two-tone paintwork of the time, and sold well.

The Zephyr/Zodiac range had continued getting larger and more comfortable in the background, quietly sprouting fins as the fashion of the day required. The transatlantic-styled Ford Classic/Capri of 1961 was a rare sales disaster for Ford, and in 1967 the all-conquering

Escort arrived to take over from all the other small Fords. It would go on to become the longest-running Ford UK model name, with no fewer than five different marks being produced before it was eventually replaced in 1999 by the Focus.

1962 saw a new medium-sized car for Ford, the Cortina. Along with the Escort, these two models would become the commonest cars on British roads of the late 1960s and the 1970s. Only the BMC 1100/1300 range came close to

Left: The 'house' styling of the Ford Scorpio (foreground) and Sierra (this one a 1987 Sierra Sapphire 2000E) was clearly carried over from the Escort seen on the previous page.

Above right: The Ford Pilot (this is a 1937 model) was a scaled-down version of the American V8 range; the latter did not sell well in Britain.

Below right: The basic Sierra (the LX version is pictured) gave birth to the fiery Cosworth model, motor-racing legend and most-stolen car in the UK in the 1990s.

equalling their sales in the early days, and that threat faded in the early 1970s with the arrival of the Austin Allegro.

A comprehensive works rally and race programme was to be built around both models, with Lotus building a special performance version of the Cortina using light panels and their own engine, while even more exotic BDA engines found their way under the bonnets of rally Escorts. There were more humble GT-badged versions for road use, and boy racers everywhere fitted ludicrously large exhaust pipes and dreamed of becoming rally drivers.

1969 saw the launch of Ford UK's first cult car, the Capri. Based on Cortina underpinnings, the Capri wore a sporting coupé body offering cramped seating for four and was, according to the advertising, 'The car you always promised yourself'. Later versions grew to make use of the 3-litre V6 from the Granada, and later still a 2.8-litre fuel-injected engine.

The Cortina died in 1982, to be replaced by the curvy Sierra, which gave rise to the fearsome Sierra RS Cosworth. Fitted with an excessive rear spoiler and a Cosworth Engineering-modified turbocharged engine, it went on to win numerous motor races, and to become the number-one target for car thieves everywhere.

With Ford cars the world over now all looking more or less the same, the days of models for the UK market alone are gone. Fords now look like all the other cars on the road: dependable and reliable, if a little dull. And so into the new century.

Humber

Manufactured: 1899 to 1976

The Name: The company was named after its founder, Thomas Humber.

The Badge: Humbers wear a simple 'Humber' script badge.

History: Like many of the early car makers, Humber started as a manufacturer of bicycles. His company had a brief flirtation with the three-wheel Pennington car before using his own designs. His early experiments were wide and varied. Both three- and four-wheeled designs were tried, and his first car was a simple 3hp model, followed by a 4hp model powered by a De Dion engine.

On Great Occasions
HUMBER
Takes Pride of Place

A PRODUCT OF THE ROOTES GROUP

London Showrooms & Export Division : Rootes Ltd., Devonshire House, Piccadilly, London, W.1

The first design to make Humber famous was the little Humberette of 1903. It featured a two-speed gearbox, and was powered by a 600cc De Dion engine. The car had an open platform to seat two people in comfort as long as it didn't rain, and as long as they avoided dusty roads. At this time windscreens were considered a dangerous inconvenience in the rain and an obstruction to the view in the dry.

There were two Humber factories in the early days, one at Beeston, Nottinghamshire, the other in Coventry. The up-market Humbers were built at Beeston, while the more pedestrian models emerged from the Coventry factory. The company was producing a wide range of models before the First World War brought things to a halt. By this time the Humberette had grown to 998cc, the range was topped by a 6.3-litre grand tourer, and everything was being built at the Coventry factory.

In the aftermath of the war, Humber managed to acquire Hillman cars and commercial-vehicle builders Commer to enhance its range and increase its market share.

As the 1920s drifted into the 1930s, the Humber range was dominated by up-market luxury saloons that put the emphasis on comfort and style over performance. The famous model names of Snipe and Pullman were heard for the first time in 1930 on a new range of six-cylinder cars, and would live with Humber until the 1960s.

In the face of the financial difficulties caused by the Depression, Humber was taken over by

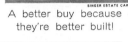
Above: By 1959, Humbers are advertised with other Rootes Group models – Sunbeams, Hillmans and Singers.

Below left: This 1948 Humber advertisement plays rather obviously on the fact that Humbers were widely used as staff cars during and after the Second World War – most famously by Field Marshal Montgomery.

the Rootes Group in 1929. Rootes kept Humber at the luxury end of the market, and by the time the Second World War began the whole Rootes range was led by the 4.1-litre Super Snipe. Humber's big, technically advanced cars would go on to become a favourite staff car with the British Army. Airfix immortalized one in its early days with a model kit of Field Marshal Montgomery's Humber staff car.

After the war, the Humber range was reintroduced with few changes. The small Hawk was powered by a four-cylinder engine, while the Snipe and Super Snipe kept the larger six-cylinder engines. All its staff-car expertise went into

the Pullman range which found great favour with both the rich and city mayors everywhere.

The cars were changed in 1948 to reflect the new fashions from America. All models sprouted air-intake grilles alongside their traditional upright chromework. The Hawk was a sleek design at the bottom of the range, while the huge Super Snipe and Pullman were joined by an even larger Imperial model. These all featured separate front wings and clung to the pre-war styling cues of running boards beneath the doors. These bigger beasts boasted seating for seven, and Imperials came with a partition to keep the driver in the front isolated from the passengers in the rear.

The range continued largely unchanged until 1958 when the new transatlantic look arrived. Two-tone paint and wide chrome grilles took away much of the dignity of the marque, but new six-cylinder engines brought them more power than most expected, and their sheer size gave them an unbeatable presence on the road. If you watch any of the black-and-white films that populate

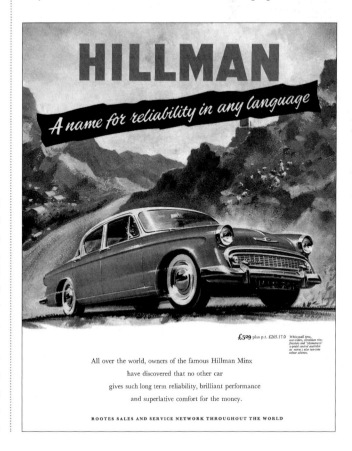

the afternoon TV schedules, you can be almost sure that someone will be driving a Humber of some sort. In its prime, the Hawk was seen as being an up-market alternative to the big Rovers, while the large models were squarely aimed at the buyers of Daimlers and even Rolls-Royces.

The early 1960s brought troubled times for the Rootes Group. Sales were falling, and the small Hillman Imp was not proving a good investment. The big Humbers were selling, but they were starting to look old and slow alongside the opposition. Desperate to generate more income, Rootes looked to its range of marques to see what could be cheaply developed. In an attempt to use the up-market Humber name to bring more customers, a new, small Humber was launched for 1963. Called the Sceptre, it used the basic body shell of the Hillman Super Minx with more chrome, four headlights and a well-apponted interior. It sold well as a luxury car for the family man, but many felt it cheapened the name.

Worse was to come in 1967. The whole range of large saloons was dropped as fashions changed and the trend swung away from big luxury cars. The last car to wear the Humber name arrived in the form of another Sceptre, except that it was now based on the Hillman Hunter. As before it featured

a luxury makeover, and this time an uprated engine was part of the package. It lasted until 1976, and sold well until it was quietly dropped by Chrysler, the new owners of the Rootes Group. Monty would not have been pleased.

Jaguar

Manufactured: 1927 to date; as Jaguar, 1945 to date.

The Name: What came to be Jaguar started life as Swallow Sidecars which, unsurprisingly, built sidecars for motorcycle combinations. In early years as a car maker the company was known as SS Cars. From 1936 their fastest models were christened SS Jaguars, the latter name after their feline good looks. When car production restarted after the Second World War, the initials SS had gained such unpleasant notoriety from their Nazi connotations that they were quietly dropped in favour of naming all subsequent models Jaguars.

The Badge: Jaguars have all worn a variation of the Jaguar 'Big Cat' badge. Early models sported bonnet mascots of the leaping cat, while safety legislation forced later models to make do with a flat badge of the jaguar's head on their bonnets and occasionally their wheel hubs.

History: William Lyons founded what was to become Jaguar Cars when he signed his first

factory lease on his twenty-first birthday in 1922 and started production of a range of sporty aluminium sidecars. Prior to this he had been

Above: A 1938 Jaguar SS 2.5-litre drop-head coupé. The company's early Standard-based saloons barely hinted at what was to come in 1948 . . .

Below: . . . when the XK range was launched at that year's Motor Show. The car was planned as a test bed for the new XK engine designed for the forthcoming big saloon. Pictured here is a 1955 XK140 drop-head coupé.

original but retained the simple 747cc side-valve engine and running gear for easy maintenance.

Not content with producing a re-bodied Austin Seven (which SS would keep in production from 1928 to 1932), Lyons soon added to the SS range by putting special bodies on the then current Fiat, Morris Cowley and Wolseley Hornet.

A rashly accepted order for 500 Austin Seven Swallows forced another move for the company as its Blackpool factory could only turn out fourteen examples per week. The centre of the

making his sidecars on a small scale in his father's domestic garage.

Orders poured in after their sidecars were seen at the Isle of Man TT and they soon outgrew their first premises. 1926 saw a move to a new site at Cocker Street in Blackpool and Swallow Sidecars (SS) was formed.

Lyons and his partner William Walmsley soon decided that the way forward was to go into car production. The traditional way to do this in the distant days of the 1920s was to buy in a chassis from a major manufacturer and re-body it with suitably unique coachwork.

They took delivery of their first new chassis in 1927, that of an Austin Seven, the most popular small car of the time and one which Lyons had driven in 1924. Besides making money, he saw this as a chance to make good all the shortcomings he had found in his own car.

The result was the Austin Seven Swallow saloon, which sported a sleeker body than the

Grace...Space...Pace... JAGUAR

The finest car of its class in the world

British motor industry at this time was Coventry, so that was where William Lyons went. With a simple move he had gone from being a small-town coachbuilder to having over 1,000 men under his control, and production blossomed.

Not content with re-bodying other people's creations, Lyons was soon bitten by the bug to produce something that was all his own. The result was the SS1, which was announced at the 1931 Motor Show.

It featured a graceful coachbuilt body over an altered Standard chassis. The Standard engine was extensively modified by Harry Weslake, an engineer who would be called upon to work his magic with many makes of cars and motorcycles in the years to come. He created a new overhead-valve cylinder head for the old Standard-designed engine which released far more power from the design and gave the cars a suitably sporting character.

The big SS1 was soon joined by the smaller SS2 based on the Standard Nine chassis, but 1935 saw the first of the models that would make SS Cars great: the SS90 (named after its top speed) sports tourer, followed closely in 1936 by the SS100.

These 2-litre and 3.5-litre open sports cars would make an impact on the motoring press well beyond anything their production figures could ever warrant. 1936 saw a factory car win a Coupe des Alpes in the Alpine Rally on its first outing, and SS100s came first and second in the 1937 RAC Rally. A much-modified SS100 managed to record a 140mph flat-out speed and a flying 125mph lap of the Brooklands circuit before hostilities brought such activities to an end in 1939.

When the war ended and it was again possible to produce new models, the now renamed Jaguar Cars took a stand at the 1948 Motor Show and displayed its traditionally styled MkV saloon and a sports tourer expected to be a stop-gap until a new big saloon was ready for production. That stop-gap car was the XK120, and another legend was born.

Initially designed as a test bed for the new 3.4-litre XK engine, orders flooded in for the car. It offered spectacular value for money, stunning styling and a remarkable turn of speed for the price (the name suggested a 120mph top speed, which subsequent tests proved to be a pessimistic estimate). Deliveries were delayed by nearly a year as Jaguar frantically retooled for the unexpected mass production and quickly added a fixed-head coupé model.

The XK120 went from strength to strength as more and more motoring writers raved about the package it offered. It grew into the more civilized XK140 in 1954 and finally the XK150 in 1958.

The big-saloon project was delayed until 1950, when the car surfaced as the MkVII, a 2-ton monster of a machine that could still top 100mph. Largely forgotten in the shadow of the more famous sports-car ranges, it was one of the finest long-distance touring saloons of its day and fathered a range of big saloons that would continue until 1970.

Successes at the Le Mans 24-hour race in 1950 with standard XK120 models led to the development of the XK120C (the C stood for competition), a title usually shortened to C-Type. These streamlined racers won the event in 1951 and 1953 (1952 saw them retire due to mechanical problems). Jaguar returned in style in 1955 with the finned D-Types which were to win the event in 1955, 1956 and 1957. Later XK150 models wore a red badge on their rear panel to commemorate the marque's success in the French classic.

While the sports-car range prospered, William Lyons set about another revolution in 1955 with the launch of his range of small saloons, the 2.4- and 3.4-litres, now known retrospectively as the MkI saloons. These were the first of what would come to be called sports saloons, and offered

transport for four in total comfort at the sort of speeds that would not have shamed most sports cars of the period. Jaguar invented the type, and executives have been fighting to own what they consider to be the flashiest model ever since.

This handsome little saloon would grow up into the MkII of 1959. A 3.8-litre engine was added to the range to make it the fastest saloon car of its day, and what many consider to be the ultimate classic car had arrived.

The sports-car range received a shake up in 1961. Plans to market the D-Type as a road car named the XKSS were shelved after a factory fire, and instead the basic technology was rethought. The result was the E-Type Jaguar – the quintessential 1960s sports car.

Left: A 1949 Jaguar XK120 fixed-head coupé. The famous XK range was offered with a fitted hardtop for those who wanted the performance but not the ruined hairstyles.

Above: The XK150, last of the family, was more luxurious that the earlier XK120 and 140 models.

Right: The fabled E-Type Jaguar arrived in 1961, and the company had given birth to another automotive legend. This is a 3.8-litre fixed-head coupé from the second year of production.

Jaguar

Above: The XJ6 saloon, voted Car of the Year when it was launched in 1968, offered a mixture of excellent ride and handling unrivalled by any other car of the time. In 1972 a version was offered fitted with the V12 engine from the E-Type and renamed the XJ12, of which this is a 1982 example.

Much like the XK120 before it, the E-Type offered a world-beating mixture of looks, performance and price. Initially available with what awas effectively the D-Type's 3.8-litre engine, it soon gained the new 4.2-litre version designed for a new saloon, and was the first Jaguar to make use of the new V12 engine in 1971. Famous personalities queued up to own E-Types, and for many years orders outstripped supply. The last of the line, a run of black convertibles with special commemorative plaques, were collector's items as soon as they left the dealers' forecourts.

The saloon-car range received a total overhaul in 1968. Both the by now gargantuan MkX saloon and the smaller, younger brothers of the earlier MkII range were all replaced by one vehicle, Jaguar's longest-running production car, the XJ6.

Scooping the coveted Car of the Year award for 1968 it set new standards for ride and refinement in a big saloon car, and was still a force to be reckoned with when production eventually ceased in 1986.

In common with most of the Jaguar saloons that had gone before, it featured acres of leather seating and a wide expanse of walnut woodwork across the dashboard. A top-of-the-range version was fitted with the V12 engine that had seen service in the E-Type to produce the XJ12 in 1972.

The mighty E-Type was not replaced until 1975, and many purists objected to the XJS V12 that took its place. A grand tourer in the great European tradition, it was faster and more comfortable than any E-Type could ever hope to be, but many felt it lacked the essential 'something' that made it a great Jaguar. But times had changed since 1961. New safety regulations were being discussed that would have banned all convertibles from the lucrative American market (the same fears would lead to the Triumph TR7 appearing with a fixed roof soon after), so it was not until 1983, when the fears were proved unfounded, that an open XJS came on the market.

After the fall of the British Leyland empire (Jaguar's owners for much of the 1970s) Jaguar eventually fell into the hands of Ford amidst cries of outrage from British enthusiasts. The arrival of a new family of V8 engines, a new XK8 sports car and an inspired XJ8 saloon silenced many of these complaints, and Jaguar looks set to begin the new century on the crest of a wave.

Behind the Wheel

Jensen

Manufactured: 1935 to 1976

The Name: The company was named after its founders, Allan and Richard Jensen.

The Badge: Jensens wear a simple winged 'Jensen' badge.

History: The Jensen story starts well before 1935, when Allan and Richard Jensen were presented with an Austin Seven by their father. Already keen motor enthusiasts, they stripped the car and turned it into a two-seater trials special. They campaigned it with such success at the Shelsley Walsh Hill Climb that they were asked to produce a similar car on a Standard Nine chassis by the chief engineer of Standard cars.

This was duly delivered, and Allan was subsequently asked to design a production version for Avon coachbuilders, who produced it as the Avon Standard.

The first car to bear the Jensen name was simply called the Jensen Convertible. It was a handsome grand tourer with four seats, soon joined by four-door versions with full saloon

Below: The Jensen V8 Interceptor convertible was a rare model, with only around sixty being made. The one pictured dates from 1974, two years before Jensen gave up car production.

coachwork. Working on the principle that a big engine equals big performance, the Convertible was powered by a 3.6-litre American Ford V8 engine, and became the first car in the world to be fitted with an overdrive as standard. This gave the car effortless performance, and it found favour with a number of celebrities, the most notable being Clark Gable. His personally designed Jensen was later put into limited production listed as the Gable Replica.

The Jensen factory was blitzed during the Second World War, and when peace returned their first product was the big PW (for Post-War) saloon. An imposing design, it was powered by a choice of Meadows, Nash or Austin engines. Sales were poor in the depressed post-war climate, with fewer than twenty being built before a new and famous name appeared at Jensen in 1949: the Interceptor. This first Interceptor was a scaled-up version of the

Austin A40 Sports design, powered by an Austin straight-six engine of 4 litres taken from the Princess range. It offered easy performance over long distances and had a slight vintage-style feel to it. Compared with the PW, it was a sales success.

The Jensen car range continued to be supported by an extensive range of commercial vehicles, and by sub-contract work for the major car manufacturers. Over the years Jensen would be responsible for final assembly of the Austin Gypsy, Austin Healey, Sunbeam Tiger and even Volvo P1800.

Their own range developed for 1953 with the arrival of the 541. Still powered by the 4-litre Austin engine, it was clothed in a sleek fibreglass bodyshell and offered 120mph performance. *Autocar* magazine claimed it was the fastest four-seat car they had ever tested. Uprated versions followed until by 1963 the elderly engine was developing 150 bhp.

The Austin engine had reached the limit of its development by the early 1960s, and no other large engine had been put forward to replace it in the Austin range. So when the Jensen brothers came to source a new unit to power their next design, they looked across the Atlantic.

The controversially-styled C-V8 arrived in 1963. It featured wildly slanting headlights in a bulbous glassfibre body loosely based on the 541. Inside, the car was well equipped, and under that bonnet lurked a Chrysler 5.9-litre V8 engine

(which would grow to 6.2-litres for 1965). Awesome 140mph performance was available, only slightly tamed by a limited-slip differential and powerful disc brakes. There was even an experimental four-wheel-drive version on the Jensen stand at the Motor Show. This would never make it into production, but the concept would reappear in the future.

The ugly-ducking C-V8 was replaced for 1966 by the sleek, Italian-styled Interceptor range. It retained the Chrysler V8 engine (in sizes ranging from 6.2 to 7.2 litres, depending on the year) and offered exceptional performance for the time.

The interior was sumptuous, with only the likes of Jaguar coming even close to providing the sort of style and comfort that it offered. As a Continental tourer, the Interceptor truly had few rivals. As the years passed it was joined by a convertible, and briefly a coupé version. But there was an even more ingenious vehicle hidden among the Jensen line-up in 1966: the groundbreaking FF.

Called 'the safest car in the world' by the motoring press, the FF featured a four-wheel drive system and revolutionary Dunlop Maxaret anti-lock brakes. The FF stood for Ferguson Formula, the four-wheel-drive unit manufacturers. The system apportioned drive to whichever wheel was losing traction via a viscous coupling mounted centrally. Modern mass-produced cars are only now catching up with the FF.

The fuel crisis of the early 1970s made the big, thirsty Jensens difficult to sell, so they looked towards other markets. Donald Healey, the man behind the cars that bore his name, and later the Austin Healey range, was appointed to the board to design a new sports car. The result was the Jensen Healey.

Powered by a new Lotus twin-cam engine, it was a square-sided car with curiously anonymous styling. Performance and handling were praised in the press, but quality-control defects in early cars and persistent problems with the Lotus engines led to poor sales. An estate version called the GT was briefly available, but the widely publicized build-quality problems had done too much damage.

American safety legislation and ever-falling sales led to Jensen slipping into receivership in 1975. Car production ceased in 1976, although the service and spares department continued. The company recovered briefly in the late 1980s when Interceptor production was restarted by the service and spares division. They used updated versions of the Chrysler engines, and retained the famous hand-built quality and style. But the price was high, and only a handful found buyers.

Lancia

Manufactured: 1907 to date.

The Name: The company was named after its founder, Vincenzo Lancia.

The Badge: *Lancia* means lance in Italian, and the badge depicts the company name either impaled on or flying from a lance.

History: Vincenzo Lancia was born into a well-off family that ran a canning business. He showed mathematical aptitude and an affinity for mechanics from an early age, and his father had him apprenticed as an accountant with the importers of British Rudge motorcycles.

The importers, Giovanni Ceirano, were beginning to produce their own motorcycle designs around this time, and young Lancia must have taken a keen interest.

The company was taken over by Fiat, and at the age of eighteen Lancia found himself appointed to the position of the company's chief inspector. He also made a friend of the Fiat group's secretary, Giovanni Agnelli.

Above left: The Interceptor convertible offered effortless high-speed touring for four from a large American V8 engine, but the engines' thirst and poor emission control were to contribute to the company's downfall.

Right: Described as a 'revolutionary phenomenon in automotive engineering', the Lancia Lambda of 1922 (this is a 1928 model) featured independent front suspension at a time when beam axles were still the norm with other manufacturers.

When Fiat decided to race their designs to gain publicity, Lancia was offered a drive in the works car. In July 1900 he won his class at Padua, with an identical Fiat coming second. Impressed by his success, Fiat made him a regular driver, and over the next few years he found himself behind the wheel in the British Gordon Bennett races, the American Vanderbilt Cup and at the French Grand Prix. A steady stream of wins made Lancia a popular man with his Fiat masters.

In 1906, Lancia decided he wanted to enter car production for himself. The first car appeared in 1907 in the form of the 12hp Tipo 51, powered by a four-cylinder side-valve engine. A six-cylinder model followed in 1908, but sales of the four-cylinder were so great that there was insufficient capacity at the plant to build both. The larger car was quietly dropped.

Lancia moved to much larger premises in Turin in 1911, and there he launched the advanced 4-litre 20-30hp Delta model, quickly joined by the 5-litre Eta. Both were generously proportioned tourers for the rich, but the early signs of the state-of-the-art cars to come were there to see.

In 1918, V8 and tightly angled V12 engines were launched, although the latter never made

it into production. Well ahead of his time, Lancia was also considering monocoque construction when separate-chassis construction was the only method in general use. Inspired by the way a ship's hull was self-supporting, Lancia made use of this technology in the V4-engined Lambda of 1922. It was fast – almost 70mph – and offered

Left: A 1938 Lancia Aprilia. Introduced the year before, the Aprilia/Ardea range enhanced Lancia's reputation with their light weight and sparkling performance.

Right: The complex Aurelia model of the 1950s offered rapid performance and a tight handling package in a sharply styled body shell.

Behind the Whee

vast amounts of interior room. There was also independent front suspension when beam axles were still the order of the day with other manufacturers. One German magazine described it as being a 'revolutionary phenomenon in automotive engineering'.

The Dilamba V8 was launched in 1929 to tempt richer customers, and a wide range of stunning body styles were available to order. Even with the heaviest styles the 4-litre engine gave energetic performance, and the sporting name of Lancia was suitably reinforced.

In the Depression years of the 1930s, Lancia made use of his earlier work with monocoque construction to launch the innovative Augusta. Such was the demand for the little V4 car that a plant was established in France to help with production. By the time the model was dropped in 1937 over 15,000 examples had been produced.

Yet another advanced car arrived for 1937, the aerodynamic Aprilia. With an enlarged V4 engine, it offered fully independent suspension to all four wheels, a lightweight stressed body shell, inboard brakes to make the best of the ride over rough roads, and a top speed of 80mph.

Lancia himself died in 1937, and his wife took over the presidency of the company. After its factory was shelled during the Second World War, Lancia moved to Bolzano, leaving its old Turin factory to be used for commercial-vehicle production after it was rebuilt.

The car range was overhauled in 1950 with the arrival of the complex V6-engined Aurelia. Much like its forebears, the Aurelia was a light, advanced car with sparkling performance. It offered excellent handling, and in open spider form it was as close as the early 1950s would ever get to offering a practical sports car. The range was replaced by the larger Flaminas in 1957, which offered much of what had gone before in a handsome body shell styled by Pininfarina (a well-known Italian stylist of the time) and boasting much more powerful versions of the V6 engine.

With financial problems looming after an energetic racing programme, the Lancia racing team was passed to Ferrari, and Fiat started to take an interest in the company.

As the 1960s drifted towards the 1970s, Lancia launched the smaller Flavia range. The V4 engines were back, now more complicated than ever, making them unpopular with garages outside the Lancia franchise and with DIY mechanics. That aside, the cars still offered excellent road-holding and performance from a

Left: The Lancia Monte Carlo (this is a 1983 example) was the Fiat X1/9's bigger brother, coded the X1/20 by Fiat. Problems with the brakes led to production being halted for a time in 1978.

light, aerodynamic body shell. The unusual exhaust note also marked the Flavia out from other cars on the road, which was a selling point in many markets.

The last of the 'real' Lancias was the Fulvia. Basically, it was the Flavia underneath a new body shell, but there was also a very limited-production Zagato coupé version, and a tuned HF (high fidelity) version with stripped specification for prospective racers.

Fiat took over the Lancia company in 1969 and allowed it to pour money into its rally programme. Based on the lightweight Fulvia, Lancia developed the Stratos rally car. Powered by the Fiat-built Ferrari Dino V6 engine, it went on to win the World Rally Championship from 1974 to 1976.

The Fiat influence was seen in the new Beta range of 1972. The distinctive V4 engines were replaced by the Fiat twin-cam four-cylinder engine, although the top-of-the-range Gamma coupé still boasted a flat-four engine designed by Lancia engineers.

The Beta was the beginning of serious trouble for Lancia. Disastrous rust problems led to a massive recall that destroyed the company's reputation all over Europe. Even the handsome mid-engined Monte Carlo coupé could not save its name.

The new Delta range of 1980 was based on the floorpan of the Fiat Strada (or Ritmo, if you lived in Italy). It was powered by uprated versions of the Fiat twin-cam engine and won the Car of the Year accolade in 1980. Despite looking like a totally conventional hatchback family car, a fire-breathing Turbo variant with four-wheel drive went on to win all the World Rally Championships from 1987 to 1992.

The lower end of the market was covered by the tiny Y10, again powered by a small Fiat engine, and very briefly there was a Ferrari-powered version of the new big saloon in the form of the 8.31 Thema.

Now firmly under the wing of Fiat, Lancia forges ahead with re-bodied versions of most of the Fiat range. Where Alfa Romeo covers the sporting requirements of Fiat, Lancia is their up-market wing. And with old worries about rust laid to rest, it looks as if one of the oldest names in Italian motoring has a bright future once more.

Maserati

Manufactured: 1926 to date.

The Name: The company was named after its founders, the Maserati brothers.

The Badge: The trident badge is derived from the statue of Neptune standing in the square of the city of Bologna.

History: In time-honoured Italian fashion, the Maserati brothers started out racing other people's cars and motorcycles before deciding to go into production for themselves in 1926. Their first design was a lightweight 1.5-litre racing car, which managed a class win in the 1926 Targa Florio race in the hands of one of the brothers.

Straight-eight and V16 engines followed, and soon the Maseratis began to think about building road, as opposed to purely racing, cars. Production of these early road cars was tiny, however, as the family were much more interested in the racers. Those that did emerge were lightly built sports cars more dedicated to speed than comfort.

In 1937, Adolfo Orsi purchased the company and moved it to Modena. He forced the Maseratis into designing their first true production car (although numbers were so limited it could hardy be called a production car), a Pininfarina-styled design designated the A6-1500.

The Maserati brothers had signed a ten-year agreement with Orsi when he took control, and when it expired they returned to Bologna and founded Osca cars. As a result, Orsi took on a new designer for the Maserati company in the form of Gioacchino Colombo, a man who had previously worked with both Alfa Romeo and Ferrari. He designed the immortal 250F Maserati Grand Prix car that went on to become one of the most successful of the 1950s. All the great names of the 1950s drove them, and Juan Fangio won a World Championship in one in 1957.

In the face of mounting debts (road-car sales were minuscule) Maserati launched a new road car in an attempt to regain profitability. The 3500GT was announced in 1957, and to save more money Maserati announced their withdrawal from the racing scene. They then promptly launched the famous 'Birdcage' Maserati racing cars, so named because they were built over a framework of small-diameter tubes. They also launched a V12 engine used by Cooper cars to win several Grand Prix races.

The 3500GT was a handsome coupé with very rapid performance. It was replaced by the

Below left: The Ferrari-powered Lancia Stratos of the 1970s, by when both Lancia and Ferrari had come under Fiat's ownership. The Stratos rally cars won no fewer than five Monte Carlo Rallies.

Right: Introduced in 1972, the Merak was a cheaper, Citroën-engined Maserati that was designed to bring new people to the marque. The car was a sales success, and it remained in production into the 1980s.

even more rapid 500GT for 1959, which was powered by a lightly detuned version of their V8 racing engine. Four twin-barrel carburettors were standard on early models, and the top speed of 170mph was incredible for its time.

The same V8 was used in the revolutionary Quattroporte (four doors) of 1963. With over 4 litres of power available, the Quattroporte broke with tradition and was a full four-door saloon car as opposed to the more usual two-plus-two design with two doors and a coupé body. Now a sufficiently wealthy family man could take the whole family with him when he went away on holiday without crushing the kids into cramped back seats. For a time, it was the fastest four-door car in the world; indeed, with well over 150mph available, it could hardly be described as being slow, even today. Its basic mechanics went on to form the core of a more conventional two-door coupé in the form of the Mexico for 1966.

The V8 engine was fitted to a sleek, long-nosed body for 1966 to create the dynamic Ghibli (named after an Egyptian wind) in direct competition with Ferrari's Daytona model. Styling was by Ghia, and at 150mph it was one of the fastest production cars of its generation.

In 1969, Orsi sold a controlling interest in Maserati to Citroën, which was looking for an engineering company to help design a new large car and engine for its range. The result was the futuristic Citroën SM, powered by the Maserati-designed V6 engine. Orsi handed his remaining interest in Maserati over to Citroën in 1971.

With the fuel crisis of the early 1970s putting big dents in the sales of all large-engined cars, Citroën soon looked to selling Maserati. When there was no interest it announced that it would have to put the company into liquidation. The bold move led to a bid from Alejandro de Tomaso, backed by an Italian Government agency.

For 1971 Maserati made a move into the exotic market with the Bora. A 4.7-litre version of the V8 engine was mounted in the middle of the car for better weight distribution and handling. Like all exotics of the time it was strictly a two-seater, and there was very little space for luggage. Compensations came in the form of the exhaust note, swift performance, a top speed of 160mph and a 0-60 time of 6.5 seconds. A cheaper version using a Citroën engine was launched in 1972 in an attempt to generate more sales. Called the Merak, it became a sales success and outlived its parent car by three years.

The de Tomaso influence appeared in 1976 in the form of the Kyalami. It used a lightly modified de Tomaso Longchamps body shell with the Maserati V8 in place of the usual Ford engine. Sales were dismal, even though the car offered the same rapid performance as the rest of the range.

In an attempt to bolster sales, Maserati made a move into the mainstream of the car market with the Bi-Turbo in 1981. A quietly styled four-door saloon, only the trident badge on the grille gave away that it was a Maserati. There were no extravagant fins or wide wheels on this Maserati. Powered by a V6 engine, it featured no less than two turbos (hence the name) to give it the urge a Maserati deserved. The interior was comfortable, and while not as fast as the exotics that kept it company in the Maserati range, it was fast enough to give most road cars of the time a run for their money. Better-developed versions followed in 1983 that offered even more performance, and a handsome convertible arrived in 1984.

Further financial troubles brought on by falling sales and questions over build quality led to Fiat taking over the Maserati concern in 1993. Eager to get the marque back into profit, they instigated a rapid refreshing of the model range. The Bi-Turbo model was given a facelift and reborn as the new Ghibli, and a new Quattroporte saloon was rushed into production. Larger engines quickly followed, and after the doldrums of the 1980s Maserati is again a force to be reckoned with in the world of exotic sports cars.

Mercedes-Benz

Manufactured: 1901 to date.

The Name: Mercédes was the name of the daughter of Emil Jellinek, one of the Daimler company's financial backers.

The Badge: The three-pointed star was derived from the three types of machines powered by the company's engines – motor cars, ships and aeroplanes.

History: Gottlieb Daimler set up an engineering company with Wilhelm Maybach in 1882. In 1883 they designed and produced the world's first internal-combustion engine (there are other claims as to who was the first, but better men than I have tried to sort out the truth).

Their revolutionary new invention was fitted to a carriage in 1886, and the first horseless carriage was born. From this humble beginning come all the cars we have today, and this single invention has arguably had more impact on the way we now live our lives than any other.

The Daimler Automobile Company was founded at Cannstadt in 1890, but Daimler died in 1900, and his place was taken on the board by Emil Jellinek, an early motoring enthusiast with money to put into this new venture. Jellinek had a daughter called Mercédes, and for licensing reasons her name was adopted on all Daimlers supplied to the French market, while all German-built Daimlers were to become known as Mercedes from the 1902 season.

Jellinek had Daimler build their first high-performance 35hp model for 1901, a four-cylinder machine with sporting performance for the time. The range prospered and grew steadily before

Right: During the 1920s the big Mercedes tourers vied with the likes of Bentley for the wealthy European clientele. Pictured is a 1927 S Model Sports.

the First World War forced a halt to all civilian car production. During the war, the company built supercharged aero engines, and from 1921 the experience and technology from them was applied to their road cars.

Ferdinand Porsche became the company's chief engineer in 1922, but the recession that followed the war forced Mercedes into a merger with Benz, to create the company we know today as Mercedes-Benz. Porsche remained as the head of engineering for the new company, and he carried on with the Mercedes trend towards supercharging.

Alongside a range of tough but unremarkable saloon cars, he launched the K sports-racing car in 1926, and this grew into the almost mythic SS range of 1928. This was a big touring car aimed directly at the same market occupied by the British Blower Bentley. The SS also wore a super-charger, activated by a switch under the throttle pedal. When the pedal hit the switch the supercharger cut in with a howl and the car rapidly accelerated. Already equipped with a 7-litre six-cylinder engine, it developed 200 bhp when the supercharger was in use.

When Porsche moved on in 1928, the supercharged cars became more refined, and a range of smaller cars using rear-mounted Porsche-designed engines was launched. The first signs of his later Volkswagen designs were to be seen in these little cars.

Mercedes went Grand Prix racing at the insistence of Adolf Hitler, and its cars were nearly unbeatable in the late 1930s. Early models used a straight-eight engine that was also used in later SS models, followed closely by a V12, and finally a V8. The latter had to be designed very quickly as the international racing rules had been

Below left: Mercedes was making luxury tourers long before the Benz name was added to their badge in 1926, as this 1912 Tour Wagen shows.

Right: The cover of a Mercedes brochure from the late 1940s, extolling the virtues of the company's 220 range of 6-cylinder cars.

TYP 220

MERCEDES-BENZ

EIN SECHSZYLINDER MIT TEMPERAMENT UND KOMFORT

changed in an attempt to give other manufacturers a chance against the state-funded Mercedes team.

Production was very slow to restart after the Second World War. The company's factories had been extensively bombed, and were now in different Allied zones of occupation. The first cars to creep back off the production lines were the 170 range of saloons. At the bottom of the range before the war, it was the best Mercedes could offer to its cash-starved German customers. It was joined by a larger 180/190 model and a 220 limousine, while a fast 300 model topped out the range in 1954. The 300 was an attempt to relive the glories of the 1930s SS models, and also signalled the return of Mercedes to the race track.

After a brief excursion with their pre-war cars, Mercedes raced the 300SL, the famous gull-wing design with its lift-up doors. Powered by the six-cylinder engine from the 300, it quickly established itself as being the car to beat in racing circles. It was simplified for mass production, and became the first Mercedes to feature fuel injection. A handsome convertible was added later in production, and 300SLs are

some of the most sought-after classics on the road today.

The well-known coupé range arrived in 1963 in the form of the 230, a good-looking coupé or convertible that found particular favour in the United States. Its engine would grow steadily over the years to cope with the power-sapping American emissions legislation.

The standard Mercedes range moved quietly on in the background behind its range-topping models. The company established a reputation for building tough, comfortable and frequently fast saloon cars. Model numbers were often reused, and soon only the imposing grille was distinctive. By the mid-1970s only an aficionado would truly tell you what lurked under the bonnet of most Mercedes.

An exception to this was the mighty 600, designed to take sales from the likes of Rolls-Royce, Cadillac and Lincoln. It was a vast car powered by a 6.3-litre V8 engine (it would later grow to 6.9-litres). Everything that could be was power assisted, and the basic model weighed in at 48.7 cwt and was 18 feet long. A special Pullman version that seated nine people was over

20 feet long and could take up several parking meters when parked. Arguably never bettered, the 600 lasted from 1962 until 1981.

As the 1970s turned into the 1980s the Mercedes range was treated to more smoothly curved body shells. Even the big square grille gained rounded edges, and in some later versions it was actually faired into the bonnet. But always the three-pointed star was prominently displayed where it would be seen in the rear-view mirror of the car ahead.

The Mercedes supercharger returned to the range of cars in 1996 with the launch of the SLK, a small (for Mercedes at least) two-seater convertible with a remarkable folding metal roof rather than a conventional hood. Waiting lists blossomed, and it seemed that Mercedes had done it again.

In May 1998 Mercedes' parent company, Daimler-Benz, entered a partnership with American automobile giant Chrysler. Their stated aim was to share technology and development costs of new designs. What this merger will give birth to remains to be seen.

Behind the Whee

MG

It's the new T.D. Midget!

... with these exciting new features — independent front wheel suspension for smoother riding; tougher, roomier body; disc wheels ... wider tyres for extra grip and control. The mid-century 'Midge' is going to win friends and influence people from Hollywood to Monte Carlo. £445.0.0 Ex Works plus £124.7.3 Purchase Tax.

Safety MG fast!

THE MG CAR COMPANY LTD., SALES DIVISION, COWLEY, OXFORD
Overseas Business: Nuffield Exports Ltd., Oxford and 41 Piccadilly, London, W.1

Manufactured: 1923 to date.
The Name: MG stands for Morris Garages.
The Badge: The initials MG were set in a suitably fashionable Art Deco octagon way back in 1923, and has remained the same.
History: The Morris Motor Company was one of Britain's largest motor manufacturers in the early 1920s. It produced the best-selling Morris Oxford, popularly known as the Bullnose Morris after the shape of its radiator. William Morris, the company's founder, also owned a number of retail garages. One of these was called Morris Garages, a group in the Oxford area to which he appointed Cecil Kimber in 1922.

Kimber quickly set about designing more sporting bodies for the basic Morris cars. These were sold at a premium through their own dealerships, and Kimber soon made a decision that would reach down the years. He built six small two-seater sports cars on the Morris Cowley chassis, and these are regarded as being the first MGs. The larger MG Super Six followed in 1924, based on the bigger Morris Oxford chassis.

Morris sanctioned a new factory at Cowley to build MGs in 1927, and made the concern a

Above left: Big, straight-eight-engined luxury cars like this 1937 Type 320 were Mercedes's staple diet before the Second World War interrupted production.

Below far left: The Type 300S roadster set the scene for the all-conquering 300 gull-wing racing cars of the 1950s.

Below left: The 230 coupé — this is a 1965 230 SL — enjoyed a long life with successively larger engines and different designations.

Above right: By 1950 MG's famous T series of sports cars were beginning to look dated.

Right: The original MG factory in 1930, with a healthy number of M-type Midgets on factory test before delivery to their new owners.

separate make in 1928. MG quickly outgrew this factory and moved to Abingdon in 1930, where the company would remain until its closure in 1980.

As Morris models changed, Kimber persuaded an ex-colleague to design an advanced six-cylinder engine to power the new MG 18/80 Sports Six, to be announced at the company's first appearance at the Motor Show.

The large 18/80 was partnered at the show by the first use of a name that would return many times. Enter the first Midget, based on the new Morris Minor. Both MG cars featured the now classic upright radiator grille immediately recognizable to any car-crazy schoolboy. With these new designs, production of MGs trebled for 1929.

Since private owners were using their cars extensively in competition, MG developed the 18/100 Tigress racing model. At the Brooklands track it was found to lack stamina in a 24-hour race, where a team of works-prepared Midgets easily won the team prize. Only five Tigress cars were ever built, while MG could not make enough Midgets to satisfy demand.

A record-breaking supercharged MG was designed for 1930 that resulted in vast amounts of publicity for the company. It managed a recorded 103mph and its chassis set the style for the next generation of MGs.

The supercharged cars formed the basis of the new C-Type Midget, which won the Irish TT races and went on to come first and third in the Brooklands 12-hour race. A new six-cylinder Midget, christened the Magna, was launched late in 1930, while 1932 saw the Midget revised to

Above left: The first of the MG line, as built in 1924. The car shown is known as 'Old Number One'.

Below left: From the 1930s MGs were used to form the basis of racing 'specials', like this K3 Magnette racer, for enthusiasts.

Right: Early MG models were lightly rebodied Morris designs. Even their original grilles remained largely unaltered, as can be seen from this 1925 Bullnose.

become the J2. Meanwhile an MG Magnette was launched to plug the gap in the range between the Midget and the Magna.

The Magnette was swiftly supercharged for the 1933 season and went on to win the Mille Miglia race team prize in Italy. The rest of the 1933 season was one of success wherever the MGs went, the year finishing with another win in the Brooklands 500-mile endurance race.

The next few years saw a bewildering diversification of engines and chassis styles as parts were mixed and matched between models. Competition wins became ever more commonplace, and in its 1935 catalogue MG stated: 'During the last four years, MG cars have won more races, taken more records and obtained more premier awards and gold medals than any other make of car in the world.'

Charles Kimber designed his masterpiece in 1935, the R-Type racing Midget. This featured a new and advanced chassis, a redesigned engine and fully independent suspension.

Seeing the immense amounts of publicity the MG cars were generating, William Morris decided to turn it to the good of the group, rather than just allowing one small part of his company to benefit. During 1935 he sold the Morris Garages company to his own company, Morris Cars, and set about making the best of the MG name. The extensive racing programme was halted, and most of the highly skilled staff were moved to the Morris company in Nuffield.

The 1935 Motor Show was the last one to feature 'pure' MG models. The Midget featured an enlarged engine and the Magnette was given a new body. But Morris had already decided things were to change. Out went the advanced and unique MG engines. From now on the mechanics would come directly from Morris cars, and MGs would be linked more closely to the basic Morris models to keep costs down. The days of the advanced racing MGs had come to an end.

1936 saw the arrival of the TA Midget. This marked the start of the famous T-series MGs

which would last well into the 1950s. They derived their power from far simpler engines than their predecessors, and were an immediate sales success. Even today there are still plenty of kit cars based on the shape of the T-series MGs.

The life of the lightly revised TB was cut short by the upheaval of the Second World War, but those in circulation found great popularity with RAF pilots and US servicemen. Many of the latter took their cars home with them, and when peace was declared they became the basis of the MG export boom. The TC (basically a re-badged TB) was quickly put back into production, and 20 per cent of all those made found their way to the USA. Following demands for more comfort from American customers, the TD was launched in 1949, and over 95 per cent of production was exported.

As cars from other manufacturers started to make the TD look old-fashioned, MG launched the facelifted TF in 1953. Still clearly recognizable as an MG T, it looked badly dated alongside the likes of the Jaguar XK range and, more importantly, the cheap Triumph TR sports cars.

Salvation came in the form of a production-ized MG Le Mans racing car of 1955, known as the EX-182. The Le Mans car was a re-bodied T-series car, but the new MGA took only its shape from the race car. A 1.5-litre engine was taken from an Austin/Morris saloon car, tuned, and mounted under the streamlined body shell on

Left: The immortal lines of the T-series Midgets (seen here on a 1955 TF), regarded as the archetypal 1930s sports-car shape, inspired a whole generation of kit cars.

Above right: During the war, the T series found great favour with American servicemen posted to Britain; when they went home they started the great American love affair with the British sports car.

the first new chassis since the T series was launched. An immediate success, the MGA 1500 was available as both a convertible and a fixed-head coupé. A genuine 100mph car in 1.5-litre form, the engine soon grew to 1.6 litres, and for a short time there was an infamously troublesome twin-cam model.

1961 saw the arrival of a new Midget. In fact, this was a re-badged version of the best-selling Austin Healey Sprite, which was designed around a Morris Minor engine and Austin A35 running gear.

The MGA was still selling strongly when its successor arrived in 1963. Enter the MGB, and with it production of MG cars more than doubled in that first year alone. Using the 1.8-litre version of the MGA engine and based very loosely on a current saloon floorpan, the MGB was MG's first non-chassis car. Its strength came from the welded box sections of the body rather than a fixed platform of girders and bars on to which the body was bolted. It was also the most comfortable MG to date, for the days when any car could be sold without the likes of wind-up windows were fast passing into history.

The MGC followed in 1967. Essentially an MGB fitted with a six-cylinder engine based on that of the Austin Healey 3000, it was never a

sales success, and it died without being mourned in 1969.

The saloon-car range had been selling away quietly in the background all this time, getting

The family car . . . . . with a sporting heart

THE

ONE AND

A QUARTER

LITRE

SALOON

For fathers who've retained their youthful craving for sports motoring, MG have made the 1¼ Litre Saloon. This is a handsome and smooth-mannered car in town, and a real devil for speed in the open. Mrs. Sportsman plus three children can sit and stare as the world sweeps by at a comfortable 60 m.p.h. or a masterly 75. This performance (with power in reserve) is one of the advantages of having a 1,250 c.c. MG sports engine in a compact saloon body!

Features include . . .
Wish-bone type independent front wheel suspension
Piston-type hydraulic dampers
Powerful hydraulic brakes
Adjustable, direct acting, rack and pinion type steering
Unusually pleasing walnut facia panel
Finest grade leather upholstery

THE M.G. CAR COMPANY LTD., SALES DIVISION COWLEY, OXFORD

London Showrooms: University Motors Ltd., Stratton House, 80 Piccadilly, W.1
Overseas Business: Nuffield Exports Ltd., Oxford and 41 Piccadilly, London, W.1

Right: Advertisement for the 1953 MG 1.25-litre saloon – a badged Morris rather than a true MG.

closer and closer to their Austin/Morris brothers, until the last Magnette was an Austin Cambridge with a large chrome grille and a lightly tuned engine. The final gleaming was the MG 1100/1300, based on the popular front-wheel-drive saloons of the time. Good sellers all, but nothing like what had gone before.

The MGB was put to rest in 1980 after all the available funds since the 1970s had been put into the Triumph sports-car range to launch the TR7. The MGB had been left to soldier on until it failed to sell well enough to be worth making, when it was quietly put out of its misery. Plans to badge some TR7 models as MGs were abandoned, and when the MGB came to a halt the Abingdon factory was closed down.

The MG name remained dormant until 1982, when it was resurrected on a performance version of the new Austin Metro hatchback. A turbocharged MG Metro soon followed, and in due course it was joined by MG versions of the larger Austin Maestro and Montego ranges. Turbo versions of both followed, each with performance worthy of the MG name, even if the purists objected.

The works rally programme gave birth to the fastest MG of them all, the Metro 6R4. While technically based on the roadgoing Metro, its only real link to the road car was that it was vaguely (and I do mean vaguely) the same shape. Powered by a 3-litre V6 engine mounted where the back seats should have been, it featured four-wheel drive and a unique engine that put out anything between 250 and 400 bhp, depending on the state of tune.

There was life yet in the MGB, however. Faced with demands from enthusiasts restoring their old MGBs, British Motor Heritage (the classic wing of the Rover Group) started making new body shells from the original tools on a limited basis. These were marketed as a spare part, but enthusiasts soon started building new cars from scratch.

Rover were inspired by this and quickly developed the MG RV8 for the thirtieth anniversary of the MGB's launch. It was an expensive, hand-made MGB fitted with the Rover V8 engine and suitably modified to cope with the extra power. Full leather upholstery and all the trimmings were standard on this limited-production vehicle, most of which went to Japan.

1995 saw the launch of the first new 'real' MG sports car since 1962, the MGF. Featuring a mid-mounted engine, it went and handled as well as the MG name deserved and received a warm welcome from the enthusiasts. There is clearly still life in this great marque.

Morgan

Manufactured: 1910 to date.

The Name: The company was named after its founder, HFS Morgan

The Badge: Morgan cars wear a simple winged 'Morgan' badge with the model number worked into a vertical bar running through the horizontal wording.

History: HFS Morgan was born in 1884 into a family of church ministers. Showing an early interest in mechanics, he studied at the Crystal Palace Engineering College, London and served his apprenticeship with the Great Western Railway. His first motoring enterprise came when he purchased a garage at Malvern Link and started a car-hire business alongside a Wolseley dealership.

Encouraged by a lecturer at the local college, Morgan started to design simple cars of his own. These early cars were lightweight single-seat vehicles with three wheels and powered by proprietary engines. His first designs used Peugeot V-twin engines and featured the twin wheels at the front rather than at the rear, as is modern practice. This resulted in a more stable design than the modern Reliant arrangement. Power was put on the road through the rear wheel via shaft drive at a time when chain drive was still a common fitment. With the power going to the rear wheel, it was also possible to build independent front suspension into the design for a comfortable ride and better handling.

Morgan set up his factory in 1910, using capital loaned by his father, and he took his first stand at the Olympia Motor Show later that year. Now powered by JAP engines (still V-twins), a two-seater soon joined the range. Sales soared until Morgan was producing nearly 1,000 cars a year by the outbreak of the First World War.

After the war Morgan launched a four-seat version of his three-wheeler, and an energetic competition programme kept the cars in the public eye. A move of premises in 1923 saw Morgan arrive at the factory near Malvern which they still occupy today.

With the launch of the likes of the Austin Seven and other small, cheap cars, sales of the relatively crude three-wheelers started to decline during the 1930s. To counter this, the first Morgan four-wheeler arrived in 1935. Powered by an enclosed Coventry-Climax engine, the 4/4 (four

Below left: A 1973 MGB GT. The MGB was the marque's longest-serving production model, with a run of twenty-seven years from 1963 to 1980. Only the Triumph Spitfire outlived it within the British Leyland stable.

Right: The three-wheeled Morgan cars were the first step into sports-car ownership for several generations of motorists. This 1933 Super Sports model, with a 1094cc JAP water-cooled V-twin engine, lowered chassis and 3-speed gearbox, was its present owner's first car in 1956.

cylinders, four wheels), looked very much like the MG sports cars of the day. The new 4/4 was much more a car for the driving enthusiast, rather than for the niche market occupied by the earlier three-wheeled designs.

After the usual production hiatus caused by the Second World War, Morgan resurfaced in 1946 with its pre-war range intact. A Plus 4 joined the four-wheeled range in 1950, powered by the

Standard Vanguard/Triumph TR2 engine. With sales tumbling, production of Morgan three-wheelers was stopped in 1952.

Both 4/4 and Plus 4 models crept on through the 1950s and 1960s with only minimal changes. The engines were updated periodically, with Ford engines making an appearance, as did later versions of the TR unit. The body styles and assembly methods remained exactly as they had back in 1935.

HFS Morgan died in 1959, and the company was passed on to other members of the family, in whose hands it remains to this day.

Faced with fears that its designs were dating badly, Morgan launched the fibreglass-bodied Plus 4 Plus. It was a fixed-roof coupé mounted on an otherwise conventional Morgan chassis. Put alongside the likes of the Lotus Elan (similar price, with the option of open-air motoring) it sold poorly and was quietly withdrawn after its 1964-67 production run. Only twenty-six ever found owners.

The Plus 8 was launched in 1968. Using the usual Morgan body style and underpinnings, it was powered by the potent Rover V8 3.5-litre engine. It was far faster than anything that had gone before, and rejuvenated interest in Morgan in the American market. Engines for the rest of the range were steadily updated, with Fiat and, later, Ford engines being used alongside the V8. But the basic design still remained unchanged. The sliding-pillar front suspension gives a firm (read hard!) ride and excellent roadholding. The development of larger versions of the V8 engine have led to incredibly rapid Morgans for the 1990s, the current model being capable of sprinting from 0-60 in 5.4 seconds.

At the time of writing there is a waiting list measured in years for the hand-built Morgan cars, which is just the way the company likes it. Suggestions for increasing production to meet demand have been refuted, and the healthy demand surely means that Morgan is doing something right.

Left: The styling of the Morgan 4-wheelers, like this 1948 4/4, has remained almost constant since their introduction in 1935.

Morris

Manufactured: 1912 to 1984

The Name: Morris was named after its founder, William Morris (later Lord Nuffield).

The Badge: The original Morris badge was an 'Ox at the Ford', the symbol of the city of Oxford. This was adopted as the first Morris car was called the Oxford, and the factory was based at the village of Cowley, now a suburb of Oxford.

History: William Morris was born in 1877 and developed a love of cycling. In common with many of the early motoring pioneers he first worked with bicycles before moving on to motorcycles in 1902. He ran his own shop/garage, and as cars became more popular, Morris offered servicing for these new vehicles.

His first car was the Morris Oxford, launched in 1913 at the cost of £175. This was fondly

Everybody notices a *Riley*

Above: Riley, which Morris had taken over in 1938, were also to come under the BMC flag after the formation of that group in 1952; this advertisement dates from the following year.

Left: The Morris Oxford of 1959. By now, Austin was the senior marque in BMC, and the products of the two companies would soon be identical apart from their badges and a few details.

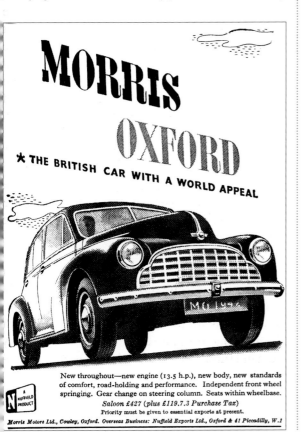

MORRIS OXFORD

★ THE BRITISH CAR WITH A WORLD APPEAL

New throughout—new engine (13.5 h.p.), new body, new standards of comfort, road-holding and performance. Independent front wheel springing. Gear change on steering column. Seats within wheelbase.

Saloon £427 (plus £119.7.3 Purchase Tax)

Priority must be given to essential exports at present.

Morris Motors Ltd., Cowley, Oxford. Overseas Business: Nuffield Exports Ltd., Oxford & 41 Piccadilly, W.1

known to as the Bullnose Morris due to the shape if its radiator, 393 finding owners in that first year.

The larger Morris Cowley (named after the village that actually housed the factory) followed in 1915 to great acclaim, despite the outbreak of the First World War that would demand munitions production from all car manufacturers.

Sales rose steadily until Morris was building nearly twice as many cars as his rivals at Austin, although he still lagged well behind the Ford Model T, which was managing annual sales well into the thousands in the UK alone.

When the horrors of war had passed William Morris was awarded an OBE in recognition of his war work. Car production restarted and saw sales rise until, by 1924, Morris was the best-selling car make in the UK. Morris managed to survive the recession of the 1920s and 1930s by pioneering the concept of hire purchase for his cars and by cutting his prices without sacrificing too much in the way of quality. Firms like the original Bentley and many others were not so lucky; some vanished for ever.

In 1922 Austin managed to deal a nasty blow to Morris by launching the 'baby' Austin Seven at a bargain-basement price just as the market was beginning to fail. Morris could produce no real opposition until the Minor of 1929, and his market share suffered accordingly. Despite falling sales, however, he still managed to purchase Wolseley cars in 1927, and would go on to add Riley to his portfolio in 1938.

To counter further the cheaper Austin Seven, Morris cut the price of his Minor in 1932 to £100. This actually drove his class-conscious customers away as they could no longer believe the car was a quality product at the new price, forcing him to increase the price again to £125.

The Minor was the best-selling Morris before war again brought production to a halt, reaching a total of nearly 200,000 cars. It had also served as the basis for the first MG Midget. Yet despite great efforts, the trials of the recession had seen the Morris share of the market dwindle, even though their millionth car was built in 1939.

After the Second World War, Morris, in common with most other British manufacturers, relaunched his pre-war range with few changes.

His next great car had to wait until 1948, when the now world-famous new Morris Minor was launched. Designed by Alec Issigonis, who would go on to design such classics as the Mini, it featured class-leading handling and up-to-date styling. Only the use of the pre-war Morris engine marred an otherwise state-of-the-art design. It was available in both saloon and convertible form, with a wood-framed estate car called a Traveller and a van appearing soon afterwards to complete the range. Morris made a rare error of judgement in describing the Minor as 'looking like a poached egg' and in taking a dislike to the car. It would go on to sell 1.25 million and remain in production until 1971.

Falling profits led to William Morris being forced into a merger with his rivals at Austin in 1952 to form the British Motor Corporation (BMC). The merger signalled the end of the individual nature of the Morris cars. Austin was soon the senior marque in BMC, even though they were supposed to be equal partners. When

The "Quality First" MORRIS

Left: Changing perceptions – no car manufacturer today would dare to have their products linked with foxhunting, as this 1951 advertisement for the Morris Oxford does.

Right: A year after the merger that formed BMC, the group's cars were still relatively distinctive. That 1953 was also Coronation Year was not lost on advertisers, either.

Far right, above: Launched in 1948, the Issigonis-designed Morris Minor was the first British car to sell more than a million examples. Issigonis went on to design the Mini.

Behind the Wheel

production designs were rationalized it was invariably the Morris designs that were dropped in favour of the Austin lines. One of the first casualties was the Morris Minor's engine. Out went the original unit, and in its place went the Austin engine from the A30. Known as the A-series engine, it was the smallest of the new group's range of engines (B and C series would follow). That the A-series engine is still with us at the start of the new century may mean that in retrospect this was a good decision, but Morris was to suffer in other areas.

The larger Oxford and executive Isis saloons were allowed to continue for a time with BMC engines before the former was replaced with a squarer version based solely on the Austin Cambridge. The large six-cylinder Isis was not replaced. BMC's big cars were now limited to the Austin Westminster and the Wolseley 6/110.

Under the BMC banner most cars were produced as both Austin and Morris versions, even

though the cars were identical. The company ran two totally separate and distinct dealership chains, which must also have caused confusion in the marketplace. The 1959 Morris Mini-Minor was launched at the same time as the new Austin Seven, both of which would soon become known as the Mini by the public. Likewise, when the front-wheel-drive revolution finally hit the family-car market, the best-selling Morris 1100/1300 range was identical to the Austin range of the same name. The same thing happened with the even larger Morris 1800 of 1966, followed by the more powerful 2200 of 1972. All were worthy and technically advanced cars that set many technological precedents, but in no way did they match the individual cars that had come before.

As the group moved on (by now known as British Leyland after a number of mergers) the Morris name was relegated to basic, 'good-value' cars in the form of the Marina, a worthy family saloon designed to take on the Ford Cortina in the fleet market, and available with a wide selection of engine sizes and trim levels. It came as saloon, estate car and even a trendy coupé with a fetching curved dashboard. The fact that this fashionable dashboard also put the radio out of sight and easy reach of the driver was conveniently forgotten in the rush of design and publicity. Despite a traditionally poor image the Marina sold 1.3 million cars and helped keep the troubled Leyland group afloat during the dark days of the 1970s. There was even a little-remembered sporting variant that made use of the MGB engine.

The Marina was replaced by the lightly restyled Ital in 1980, and the Morris name died quietly in 1984, a sad end to a great marque.

THE NUFFIELD TEAM

MAINTAINS THE LEAD IN CORONATION YEAR

MORRIS

WOLSELEY

Morris Minor
Morris Oxford
Morris Six

New Wolseley Four Forty - Four
Wolseley Six - Eighty

Riley

MG

Riley 1½ litre
Riley 2½ litre

M.G. 1½ litre Saloon
M.G. "TD" Midget

*Our tradition of service
and our reputation for value have grown through five reigns*

NUFFIELD ORGANIZATION   BMC   Overseas business: Nuffield Exports Limited
Cowley, Oxford & 41 Piccadilly, London, W.1

Packard

Manufactured: 1899 to 1958

The Name: The company is named after brothers James Ward and William Doud Packard, its founders.

The Badge: Packards are recognized less by their badge than by the shape of their radiators. These invariably had 'shoulders' on each top edge, even in the 1950s when huge chrome grilles and bumpers had become standard in the USA.

History: The Packard brothers began their activities in car making in 1899 when they rose to a challenge from Alexander Winton to improve one of his designs after they had criticized it. With their new, improved design they established the New York and Ohio Automobile Company in Warren, Ohio. The latter end of 1899 saw the launch of their first production car, the Model A.

The Model A was a well-made, if traditional, design powered by a single-cylinder engine, and continued through a change of company name in 1901 to the Ohio Automobile Company, and finally to the Packard Motor Car Company in 1902. Extra funding arrived in 1902 in the form of Detroit businessman Henry Joy who moved the company to Detroit, although the Packard brothers moved on to other enterprises.

With the advent of this extra finance new two- and four-cylinder-engined vehicles were added to the Packard line, and one managed a spirited showing in the first running of the Vanderbilt Cup races.

A new six-cylinder range arrived in 1911, as did future company president Alvin Macauley, commonly referred to as the 'only gentleman in automotive manufacture'. With its cars drifting

---

Is That Really True?

In 1931 Prince Eugène of Belgium crossed the Sahara using two Packard Eights.

When the 1930s Eight model was dropped from the Packard range after the Second World War production rights were sold to a company in the USSR, where it re-emerged as the Zis in 1946.

Left: Early Packards, like this 1908 model, soon developed the 'shouldered' radiator grille that would become their trademark.

Above right: The first of the 6-cylinder Packards arrived in 1911.

Below right: Luxury touring cars dominated the early Packard range.

slowly but steadily up-market, 1913 saw Packard launch its first model with electric lights.

1915 was a momentous year as the world's first production V12 motor car arrived on the scene in the form of the Packard Twin Six. Based around the company's well-respected V12 Liberty aero engine, it was a fast, smooth car that American President Warren Harding used to ride to his inauguration in 1920. Capable of acceler-ating smoothly from as low as 5mph in top gear, it was a magnificent vehicle many years ahead of its time.

All through the 1920s Packard was firmly set-tled as the premier marque in the USA, with agencies all over the world. By concentrating on the top end of its model range they firmly beat the likes of Cadillac and Lincoln into second and third places.

Left: In common with most expensive and exclusive cars of the day, unusual mascots are a common fitting on Packards, as this shot of the radiator cap on a 1932 900 Sedan shows.

Below: The Packard Super Eight of the late 1930s (pictured is a 1938 1601 convertible) was an inspired if slightly ungainly design. The trademark extravagant bonnet mascot and shouldered radiator are still very much in evidence.

Above right: V12 engines were a feature that gave Packard cars like this 1938 Coupé convertible a distinctive long-nosed appearance.

Below right: A 1955 Packard Caribbean convertible. The Caribbean was Packard's last flowering of excess, and the company finally died in 1958.

By the early 1930s the Great Depression was having an impact on Packard, forcing it to launch the smaller eight-cylinder 120 model in 1935 to keep it solvent. Profitable once more by 1936, it looked as though Packard had been saved. An even smaller six-cylinder model was added to the range in 1936 to widen further its customer base, while production of the larger models continued, and continued to appeal to more traditional owners.

During the Second World War, Packard built Rolls-Royce Merlin V12 aero engines under licence, and after the war the company found car sales falling in the face of the more technologically advanced competition. It had allowed itself to stagger on with straight-eight engines when most competitors had adopted the more fashionable V8 engines, and many of its designs now looked dated. In a revolutionary move Packard dropped its expensive, top-of-the-range model to con-

Behind the Whee

centrate on the lower end of the market. Cadillac quickly inherited the crown as premier make in the USA and never looked back.

A new company president in 1952, James Nance, attempted to revive the Packard reputation by moving the name back up-market. New Caribbean and Clipper ranges arrived in 1953, as did a family of limousines. Nance was determined to cut all links with what he saw as a troubled past and closed down parts of the spares operation, which had been providing much-needed cash-flow to the company. He also sought to modernize the line by buying in the Studebaker company and its well-respected V8 engine.

In the midst of all this reorganization a deadly blow was received when Chrysler purchased the coachbuilders who supplied Packard with their bodies, and quickly cut off supply.

Nance resigned in 1956 after the Packard-Studebaker combine was taken over by Curtiss-Wright, who kept the name alive by re-badging the cheaper Studebaker designs. The once great Packard marque was allowed to die quietly in 1958.

Peugeot

Manufactured: As a car maker, 1891 to date.

The Name: The company was named after its founder, Armand Peugeot.

The Badge: The lion badge was adopted for Peugeot's range of saw blades in 1858 as a symbol of strength and speed.

History: The Peugeot family started out in the ironmongery business as far back as 1810, and bicycles joined their products in 1855.

Armand Peugeot sold wood-working machinery to the Panhard company, and he was inspired by Panhard's opinion that the future lay in mechanically powered vehicles. After a brief and failed flirtation with steam power, Peugeot obtained a supply of Daimler engines. His first vehicle emerged in 1891, powered by a rear-mounted engine and using chain drive. Steering was via a boat-style tiller, and as was common at

the time, the new car looked very much like a horse-drawn carriage with the shafts removed. Five such cars won the Paris-Rouen race of 1894, taking the team prize of 5,000 gold francs. From

Left: A Peugeot Bébé 5 from 1902.

Facing page, above left: A 1976 advertisement for the 104 – not a particularly remarkable little car, but undeniably long-lived.

Facing page, above right: The '04' range were typical Peugeot fare: basic but dependable and sensibly priced. Cars like this 1971 504 estate are still being used daily all over the world, often with huge mileages under their wheels.

Below right: The 205 – this is a GR model from the 1980s – started life as a simple town hatchback but was developed into the GTI, commonly regarded as one of the finest in its class when it appeared in 1984.

1897, the company built its own engines and the Peugeot car range expanded rapidly into all areas of the new motor trade.

The first small Peugeot arrived in 1902 in the form of the Bébé. Powered by a small 652cc single-cylinder engine, it was an immediate sales success. It was partnered at the top of the range by the large six-cylinder Type 105 with an engine capacity of 11.1-litres. The latter was often found fitted with sports-style bodies and could reach speeds of 80mph under the right conditions.

After the hiatus caused by the First World War, production restarted slowly, and only in 1921 did the new Quadrillette model replace the popular Bébé. None the less, Peugeot was quickly gaining a reputation for making basic, sturdy cars with little flair but great toughness.

The Quadrillette was put under pressure by the other small cars of the 1920s, and evolved into the 5CV in 1924. Whereas before it was more of a cyclecar, the new 5CV was a proper car in the style of the Austin Seven.

The first car to use the now well-known model numbering system with an 'o' in the middle arrived in 1936 in the form of the 201, a simple, reliable car with few pretensions.

New streamlined Peugeots had been launched in 1935 after the introduction of the Citroën Traction Avant forced every other French company to look closely at its ranges. The new Peugeots were well received, but under the skin lay the usual simple, if trustworthy, mechanics.

After the Second World War, the Peugeot factories were in ruins, and it was 1948 before large-scale production began again. Their first new design was the simple 203, a handsome, aerodynamic design that stood the test of time until production ended in 1960. It was Peugeot's first monocoque design, and there were convertibles, estate cars, and even a sporting model named after the Paris dealer Darl'Mat. The 403 completed the limited range for the 1950s. A larger saloon (as indicated by the higher first number in the designation), it was the usual

uninspiring Peugeot fare that kept the French on the road for years – boring but indestructible.

The 404s came next, and were more of the same, closely followed by the lighter 204 range, which became best-sellers in the 1960s environment that smiled upon any small car. Much as before there was a full range of models available, including convertibles that actually had proper seating for four people.

Just occasionally, Peugeot produced a jewel among their more modest fare. One such was the 504 coupé. A handsome machine in either fixed-roof or convertible form, it was powered by an excellent V6 engine (a first for a Peugeot) jointly developed by Peugeot, Renault and Volvo. It went on to power the new 604 executive saloon in 1976.

Facing increasing competition from the smaller cars on the market, Peugeot launched the long-lived 104 model in 1972. Not a particularly remarkable little car, it served Peugeot well before being re-badged as a Citroën LN in 1974, when Peugeot bought that company, and went on to become the Talbot Samba when Peugeot added Chrysler UK to their group in 1977. This was the first step down the path that would see many of Citroën's later models based on Peugeot designs, and the Talbot name disappear completely.

The numbers marched on, but Peugeot had to wait until 1983 for their next big hit. The 205 hatchback arrived on the crest of the hot-hatch wave, and the GTI version was one of the best regarded. Despite a rough ride and a jerky drive in traffic, Peugeot found they could sell as many 205s as they could make.

The '06 range arrived in the 1990s, and with it came the 306. A medium-sized family hatchback, it would go on to become Peugeot's best-selling car ever. It was joined by the 406 saloon, to travelling representatives' delight (the 405 of the 1980s had started a trend towards this market), and this in turn gave birth to the good-looking 406 coupé. Such was its impact on the market that deadly rivals Ford had to rush a coupé version of their own repmobile, the Mondeo, into production.

When the people-carrier revolution came in the 1980s, Peugeot could not afford to be left behind. Their earlier offering was the seven-seater 504 estate car, which now looked very dated alongside the likes of the Renault Espace. Seeking to share production costs, Peugeot brought back the age of badge engineering by sharing the same basic design with Citroën and Fiat. Peugeot designated it the 806, Citroën the Synergie, and Fiat the Ulysses. And we all laughed at BMC in the 1960s with their 1100/1300 range with all its variants. Maybe they were just ahead of their time.

The current Peugeot range continues to sell well, and has finally dragged itself away from its dull-but-reliable image.

Left: The 405 was the first Peugeot to find success in the British 'repmobile' market traditionally dominated by Ford and Vauxhall.

Above right: A 1909 Renault Type AX. The small AX was the first in a line of compact cars that continued right through to the Renault 5 of the 1970s.

Behind the Wheel

Renault

Manufactured: 1898 to date.

The Name: The company was named after its founders, the Renault brothers.

The Badge: The badge was originally formed by intertwining the initials of the three founding brothers (Louis, Marcel, and Fernand) and their surname Renault in a geometric design.

History: The Renault brothers were born into a family famous for the manufacture of buttons. Showing an early interest in mechanics, Louis Renault designed and built a small car for his own use. A typical horseless-carriage design of the time, it was powered by a De Dion engine and featured the advanced shaft drive over the more common exposed chain used by many cars of the day.

Louis Renault's new car interested several people, and he soon received orders to build replicas. Seeing the future potential, he launched his own company in 1898 and exhibited his first cars at the Paris Motor Show later that year. He received sixty orders at the show, and Renault was on its way.

Building nearly 200 cars in his first full year of production, Louis Renault followed the lead of many other manufacturers and looked to racing to publicize his cars. A 6.3-litre racing car was developed and driven by his brother Marcel. Wins followed in the Paris-Trouville and Paris-Vienna races, but Renault pulled out of racing when Marcel was killed in the 1903 Paris-Madrid race.

By 1902 Renault was building its own engines with one, two or four cylinders. It also set a trend for mounting the radiator near the engine on the car, rather than at the opposite end of the vehicle. This did away with many long, complicated and vulnerable pipes and made the cars run more efficiently.

Early Renault models, such as this 1902 example, made their name on the race track and featured few creature comforts.

A new range of twin-cylinder engines for 1905 proved instant best-sellers, their tough nature making them popular with traders and taxi drivers who covered high mileages. Like the opposition at Citroën, Renault introduced buses and lorries, and was the first manufacturer to produce a bus with twenty-one seats, and a purpose-built taxi.

Many Renault vehicles found themselves pressed into service by the armed forces during the First World War. Over 600 Renault taxis were commandeered to transport troops to the front line during the Battle of the Marne in 1914, the action that saved Paris from capture by the Germans.

Military demands for new technology allowed Renault to expand his operation on the basis of war work. He moved into aero engines and purpose-built military vehicles that quickly found their way to the Western Front. In preparation for further German attacks, a new factory was built near Lyons. When the threat was averted, Renault retained the factory and doubled his capacity at a stroke.

After the war, Renault continued making bread-and-butter four-cylinder models, and topped its range with a mighty 9.1-litre luxury car, known as the 40CV. With the cars selling well, Renault expanded into engines for marine and railway use, as well as railway rolling stock, and became the world's largest producer of aero engines.

One of Renault's most important designs surfaced just before the Second World War. The 8CV Juvaquatre was the firm's first monocoque-construction vehicle, and offered excellent performance from a small, lightweight engine. It proved popular with family motorists, and would no doubt have sold more had not the German invasion and occupation of France halted production. After the war the commercial version continued to be made until 1959.

Left: In 1910, when this AX was built, windscreens were still considered a hindrance to vision, and so frequently did not feature on cars of the period.

Above right: The 4CV of 1945-61 made use of the rear-air-cooled-engine concept inspired by VW's Beetle.

Below right: The 8CV Juvaquatre, Renault's first monocoque design, spanned the war years and stayed in production until 1959 with a selection of engines.

Louis Renault was imprisoned as a collaborator after the war and died in prison. Under German occupation he had been forced to keep his factories operating, producing war material for the German armed forces.

The benefit of having the factories active during the war years, however, was that a new design of car was ready for production when peace was declared. With Renault now a nationalized company, the rear-engined 4CV was rolling off the production lines alongside the earlier 8CV in 1945.

The 4CV was another sales success, and lasted until 1961 with a production run of well over a million vehicles. It was another light, basic design that provided transport for the poorly paid family man.

The slightly larger Dauphine saloon was launched in 1956. This was another rear-engined saloon that again sold over the magic million mark. It was produced under licence in Brazil, and a tuned version saw the first arrival of the Gordini name on a Renault. Tuned by Amadée Gordini, these special models soon came to be an essential part of the Renault model range.

The long-lived front-engined Renault 4 replaced the 4CV in 1961. Designed as competition for the Citroën 2CV, it was a more refined but still basic design (early models had a dipstick to check fuel levels, rather than a gauge) that lived on until 1992. The 2CV lived longer, but a production run of twenty-one years is a success in anyone's eyes.

More rear-engined saloons followed through the 1960s, most with hot Gordini versions that made their name with boy racers and rally enthusiasts everywhere. Then, in 1972, Renault launched its most successful design.

The Renault 5 was perhaps the first modern supermini design. This time the engine was in the front, and the car offered front-wheel drive. The body was a spacious two-door hatchback capable of carrying four adults in comfort. The ride was supple, even if power was limited from the early 956cc versions. Later models offered more power, including a Gordini and a turbocharged version, despite infamous hot-running

problems with the turbo. For over thirty years there was a Renault 5 for nearly every sector of the market.

In 1985 Renault wrote a whole new page in the rulebook of motoring design with the Espace. The first of the 'people carriers', it offered seating for seven in a high, square-sided vehicle. Sales soared, with the only opposition coming from minibuses and the extra seats in estate cars like the Peugeot 504 and Rover Montego. Suddenly everyone wanted a people carrier, no matter how many people they actually had to carry. Other manufacturers hastily collaborated to introduce similar vehicles in their own ranges to stop Renault cornering the market.

With the market now settled and most manufacturers offering people carriers in their ranges, Renault must now be thinking where it can go for its next trend-setting design. Whatever it may be, it will be well worth waiting for.

Rolls-Royce

Manufactured: 1904 to date.

The Name: The company is named after its founders, Henry Royce and the Hon. Charles Rolls.

The Badge: The badge consists of the two Rs of the company founders' names intertwined. Early models had the lettering in red, but it was changed to black in 1933 following the death of Royce.

History: Henry Royce was an engineer, and in 1904 he designed his own 10hp car to counter the problems he found with the Decauville car he used as his personal transport.

Famed for his expertise and design principles, Royce went on to design three-, four- and six-cylinder versions of his first prototype, all the engines using the same bore and stroke dimensions. Charles Rolls was suitably impressed with the quality of the designs and prototypes and offered Royce a deal. His company would buy every car Royce could manufacture, badge them as Rolls-Royces, and market them accordingly.

Royce accepted this deal in 1904, and by 1906 the Rolls-Royce motor company was formed. That year saw the launch of the first of the cars that would make Rolls-Royce famous. The mighty 40/50 was the first car produced under the company's 'one-model' policy. It was a heavy, expensive and sophisticated car, available in chassis form only. Buyers then took the rolling chassis to their favourite coachbuilder to commission the body style of their own choice. Power came from a large 7-litre six-cylinder engine that could push the heavy car along at speeds over 50mph. That might not sound like much now, but in 1906 it was supercar performance.

This model is often wrongly referred to as the Silver Ghost. The Silver Ghost was a factory-owned 40/50 fitted with a factory-designed body. It was famous for being used in a publicity run that saw it driving from Land's End to John-o'-Groats in top gear, and it still exists today. It has become perhaps the best-known Rolls-Royce in existence.

The same chassis would find use in military circles as the basis of the Rolls-Royce armoured car, which saw extensive service with the troops of the Empire during the First World War. A tough, long-lasting design, some were still in ser-

Left: A 1907 Rolls-Royce. This particular car, 'The Silver Ghost', was a specific 40/50 used by the company for publicity purposes. Built before the adoption of the famous 'Spirit of Ecstasy', it wears an AA badge as a mascot. (Note the lack of wings on top of the badge, which did not arrive until 1911 – coincidentally the year Rolls-Royce radiators first sported the 'Spirit of Ecstasy'.)

Behind the Wheel

vice in the desert campaigns of the opening years of the Second World War.

For 1919, Rolls-Royce operated a plant at Springfield, USA. This was to allow Rolls-Royce cars to be sold in the United States without having to pay the prohibitive import taxes in place at the time. Unlike the original British cars, Springfield cars were actually available with 'standard' coachwork fitted. The Springfield works produced both 40/50 and Phantom models before the Great Depression reduced sales to such a low level that it was no longer economical to continue, and the factory closed down in 1931.

Demand for the 40/50 had been such that Rolls-Royce had been forced to move from its original Manchester premises to Derby in 1908. After the war, as the recession started to bite, a new 'small' Rolls-Royce was announced for 1922. This used a new 3.1-litre engine, again with six cylinders, but of a more advanced design than the original unit. Although aimed at people with more modest means than the 40/50, the new Twenty was still a very expensive car and well beyond the pockets of all but the wealthiest motorists.

The 40/50 was dropped in 1925, and the Twenty grew into the 3.6-litre 20/25 for 1929.

This in turn grew to 3.6- and 4.2-litre sizes before being used in the new Bentley models launched after the Rolls-Royce takeover of 1931.

The large 40/50 was replaced by the mighty Phantom range. This time the engine was a 7.6-litre six, and for the first time the radiator had the vertical polished slats that are thought of today as a company trademark–earlier Rolls-Royce models had either horizontal slats or a matt-black radiator core within a square setting. The Phantom II was launched in 1930, with numerous technical improvements and more power. This was the last car totally designed by Royce before he died in 1933 (Rolls had been killed in an aircraft crash in 1910), but the name was to go on to even greater things.

1935 saw the arrival of what many enthusiasts argue was the finest Rolls-Royce ever made, the Phantom III. In place of the usual straight-six engine there was a new V12, whose design was inspired by the company's aero engines. Aimed directly at the American manufacturers who were turning out cars with more and more cylinders

Above left: Early Rolls-Royce vehicles were sold in rolling-chassis form only. Owners then had to get them clothed by the coachbuilder of their choice. Once again, the lack of a 'Spirit of Ecstasy' mascot marks this car as being pre-1911.

Below : By the 1920s the Rolls-Royce trademark of big, luxury cars for the very rich – like this 1924 limousine – was firmly established.

common to as many versions of the cars as possible. This had the biggest impact on the sporting Bentley range, which was soon reduced to a shadow of its former self.

The new engine range was designed so it could easily be produced in four-, six- or eight-cylinder versions. This allowed the usual six-cylinder unit to be used in the cars, and the others to find homes within more commercial projects.

The first of the new range was the Silver Dawn, the first Rolls-Royce to wear a standard-pattern steel body. More prosperous customers could order the Silver Wraith which usually came with older-style coachbuilt bodies. Kings and queens could ride in eight-cylindered comfort in the new Phantom IV.

(V16 was as large as they came), it was a big, expensive car again only available in chassis form. Buyers still had to pay to have a suitable body fitted by an external supplier.

The Second World War brought production of the Phantom III to an end. Rolls-Royce turned its efforts to aero engine production at Derby, and at a new factory at Crewe. Some of the finest aircraft of the war were powered by Rolls-Royce Merlin engines, including the Hurricane, Spitfire, Mustang, Mosquito and Lancaster.

After the war, Rolls-Royce embarked on a massive reorganization of its range. It was clear that the days of expensive, chassis-only cars had passed, and the Phantom III was not revived. The plan was now to keep as many components

Is That Really True?

The only vehicle built outside the Rolls-Royce factory legally permitted to fly the 'Spirit of Ecstasy' mascot was FAB 1, Lady Penelope's pink Rolls-Royce in the TV series *Thunderbirds*.

Plans to name a Rolls-Royce the Silver Mist were hastily dropped when it was found out that the word *Mist* in German had impolite connotations.

Rolls-Royce never quote power outputs for their engines; they are always described as 'adequate'.

Above left: Early Rolls-Royce rolling-chassis frames being assembled in the company's cramped premises at Cooke Street in Manchester, *c.*1904. They moved to Derby in 1908.

Left: The first designs — this is a 'Legalimit' V8 from one of the company's own advertisements — barely hinted at the greatness that was to come for the Rolls-Royce name.

Behind the Wheel

The six-cylinder engine was enlarged for the new Silver Cloud of 1955. This was a bigger car than the earlier steel saloons, and featured the long, sweeping front wings that most people expect to see on an older Rolls-Royce.

It was the first car to carry the new V8 engine in 1959, an engine that would live on until the turn of the century. The Phantom V and VI grew and continued on into the 1980s before lack of demand caused them finally to be laid to rest in favour of long-wheelbase versions of the standard vehicles.

Monocoque construction at last arrived in 1965 in the form of the squarer Silver Shadow. Still powered by the V8 engine, it sold better than any earlier Rolls-Royce. Disc brakes were fitted all round to tame the higher performance available with the light body, and there was even variable ride-height control at both ends. A convertible version was available for the first time on one of the standard-bodied cars, and a handful of coupé versions arrived by courtesy of Mulliner Park Ward coachbuilders.

The aero-engine company that was part of Rolls-Royce drifted into bankruptcy in 1971, but as the cars continued to produce a profit, production was unaffected. The Silver Cloud became the Corniche, and the roadholding of the basic model was overhauled for 1976 to answer

complaints that it favoured a soft ride at the expense of handling. A big coupé version of the Silver Shadow called the Carmargue joined the range in 1974, but found few buyers. A big, good-looking car in the sporting mould, it was one of the few not to feature a Bentley version.

The range was steadily developed in a similar style through the recession of the 1980s, but despite rising sales in the 1990s with the new Silver Seraph model Rolls-Royce fell into the hands of Volkswagen in 1998. The Rolls-Royce name came to be owned by BMW, who were supplying engines for the new models, and they intend to set up a new Rolls-Royce company in 2003.

Above right: A Rolls-Royce light armoured car on patrol in Samaria, Palestine, in 1917, during the campaign against the Turks. The Rolls-Royce armoured car was designed for use by the Admiralty in 1914, and was still in service in India in 1945.

Right: In the early days, Rolls-Royces like this 1906 Light 20 were considered excellent competition cars. Can you imagine doing this with a modern example?

Rover

Manufactured: 1904 to date.

The Name: The original bicycle which gave the company it's name was known as 'the Rover', because it was ideal for 'roving about'.

The Badge: The Viking was adopted by the Rover company as they were the most successful rovers of their time. Some cars wore the famous Viking ship insignia, others wore a chrome-plated Viking's head, and some even featured a standing-Viking mascot.

History: The Rover company (or what would eventually become Rover) started life producing sewing machines, then followed the well-worn track of producing bicycles, followed by motorcycles, before making the leap to motor cars in 1904.

The first car was a single-cylindered 8hp model that quickly developed a reputation for being a tough design. A lighter 6hp model was introduced in 1906, and soon there was a wide range of single- and twin-cylinder models available to suit most tastes. For 1911 there was even a version that used the well-known Knight engine for those who did not trust Rover's own unit.

After the First World War, Rover resurrected its light-car range and soon added its refined 14/45 air-cooled models, which offered more comfort than many of their competitors. Expansion came quickly to Rover, and it had a wide model range when the Great Depression hit it hard.

A new general manager arrived in the person of Spencer Wilks. He examined the whole range of cars Rover was producing and made sweeping changes. He effectively retargeted the range at the ultra-conservative British middle classes, and Rover soon came to be regarded for its quality and refinement above all else. There were 10, 12, 14, 16 and 20hp versions of its stylish cars, many available in streamlined 'Speed' form to appeal to the sporting motorist. A range of larger models known as Meteors and Pilots became famous for their outstanding quality and pure luxury.

After the inevitable halt for the Second World War, Rover moved to a new factory in Solihull, since its original Coventry premises had been bombed. Rover had been running the Solihull

Left: Until the Second World War interrupted production, Rover made a range of quality two-seat tourers that would be dropped from their product line after 1948, never to return. Pictured is a late 1930s Rover Nizam.

Above right: The styling of the Rover SD1 of 1976 was modelled on the Ferraris of the day.

Below right: The Range Rover started a trend for recreational four-wheel-drive vehicles that blossomed in the 1990s to a frightening extent. Only Rover was doing it in 1970.

Behind the Wheel

plant for some time as part of the government's shadow-factory scheme and was happy to move in when hostilities ceased.

After the inevitable relaunch of its older range in 1945, the first new Rover arrived in 1949. The P4 range (universally known as 'Auntie' Rovers after a journalist's remark that driving a P4 was like visiting a favourite aunt) set new standards for the company.

The P4 was loosely based on the styling of the American Studebaker of the time, with aluminium doors, bonnet and boot lid to keep the weight down. The engines were initially derived from the earlier models, and a vast number of options were available before the range was dropped in 1964. These included a freewheel system for changing gear without dipping the clutch, electric overdrive for effortless cruising, and for the first time on a Rover, an automatic gearbox. The middle-classes loved the Rover P4 range as it offered all the class and comfort of the earlier models, coupled with a new turn of speed and level of refinement.

The company moved further up-market in 1958 with the 3-litre, or P5 as it was known at

Rover. It was a large executive car powered by a big six-cylinder engine, and found favour with mayors and ministers everywhere. It offered drawing-room comfort at high speed for four passengers. Even the Royal Family took to them, and legend has it that the Queen counts the big Rovers as being among her favourite cars.

When the heavy 3-litre started to loose its performance edge over the competition in 1967 a new 3.5-litre V8 engine – bought in from Buick in America – was slotted in to produce rapid performance to match the newly introduced coupé body style. The 3.5 officially became the

P5B (B for Buick) and the new engine could push the big car along at nearly 110mph, while acceleration was as good as most sports cars of the day. Production continued until 1973, by which time the car had been largely relegated to official functions. It remained a favourite car of government ministers everywhere, and when Margaret Thatcher started her first term in government in 1979 she arrived in a P5B. Earlier, Prime Minister Harold Wilson had had the ashtray on his personal P5 modified to accommodate his pipe.

A new generation of Rovers had arrived in 1963 with the Rover 2000, which made use of a revolutionary construction method. All the outer panels were bolted to a stressed internal skeleton, not unlike the Superleggera system, and the mechanics were hung from the same structure. The engines were a new family of four-cylinder units (the V8 would follow in 1968 to turn the car into a real sports saloon) and the rest of the mechanics were very advanced for their day. The rear brakes (discs all round) were mounted inboard of the wheels to reduce unsprung weight, and there was fully independent suspension at all four corners.

The press raved about the new Rover 2000, and it remained one of the most advanced saloon cars in the world right up until it was replaced in 1976. The car that replaced it was every bit as revolutionary as the 2000 had been to the P4 range.

The new SD1 (Solihull design 1) was a big hatchback car that brought the Rover name right up to date. Power came from the immortal V8 and a selection of straight-six engines, and for a time the V8 version was the fastest hatchback in the world. The styling was inspired by the Ferrari Daytona, and the car featured rear suspension that could be adjusted from the driver's seat to allow for the weight being carried in the boot. A heated element was built into the windscreen surround to make fitting new windscreens easier in the event of breakage. Many of the complications of the earlier P6 model had been phased out in favour of more modern methods, such as suspension by Macpherson struts in place of the original complicated De Dion system attached to a separate frame. Yet it still handled perfectly.

Once again the press praised the way the new model handled, but the modern-style interior turned its back on the wood and leather that had made earlier Rovers such an experience, and journalists found fault with it. Later models by

Behind the Whee

Vanden Plas answered this criticism, but by then it was too late.

The Rover SD1 arrived when the Rover group (or British Leyland, as it was then) was at the height of its troubles with the unions and when production standards were at their lowest. Tales of trim falling off and/or apart were common, as were water leaks and untraceable rattles. The result was that the SD1 was a great Rover that never quite made it into the big time like its predecessors.

The last fling of the SD1 came with the Vitesse of 1982. Now renamed the SE1 range in an attempt to prove that things had improved at Rover (build quality had indeed improved out of all recognition), the Vitesse used a 190bhp version of the 3.5-litre V8 engine to offer a 0-60mph time of marginally over seven seconds, and the sort of performance that took it to victory in both the British and German touring-car race series. But much of it was too little too late and Rover losses started to mount in the face of a poor public image.

In an attempt to bolster its reputation, the company approached Honda with a view to a joint venture to share development costs. The first venture was the Triumph Acclaim (see the Triumph entry, p. 129). When this proved a success the new Rover small family car, the 200, was based on a Honda design despite being built in Britain. The new big car, the 800, and the new 200/400 family car series were truly joint design exercises, yet Rover still managed to keep its cars separate from its Japanese equivalents. The Rovers returned to their traditional wood-and-chrome interiors where Honda followed more 'modern' thinking. Rover also took care to ensure it used its own world-class engines and to design its own specific variants, such as the 200 Turbo coupé and convertible. As a result Rovers frequently outsold their Honda versions in Europe, and the company's association with the Honda name led to sales in Japan, where the cars were seen by many as luxury Hondas.

Following the trials of the 1970s and 1980s Rover was acquired by British Aerospace in 1988, and they in turn put the company up for sale in the early 1990s. With a solid portfolio of cars to offer, the company was snapped up by BMW. Yet despite subsidies from the British Government, BMW sought to obtain a quick return on their investment by selling off the Rover group in 2000. To maximize their profits, the German concern split the company into several parts. The world-famous Land Rover brand was sold to Ford, while the saloon cars and MG sports cars, and the factories that built them, were sold to a consortium of British businessmen for a token £10. What the future holds for Rover only time will tell.

Saab

Manufactured: 1950 to date.

The Name: Saab stands for Svenska Aeroplan AB.

The Badge: Saab cars wear a griffin crest, symbol of the Skane district of Sweden where the Scania truck division of Saab was based; Saab retained the badge for their cars when they took the truck company over. Earlier Saab cars displayed the Saab initials over a stylized aircraft design.

History: The Saab story began in 1950 when a purely practical decision was taken to begin car production. Saab had long been a well-known producer of aeroplanes (hence the symbol on some of its car badges), especially military designs. In the years following the Second World War, demand for aircraft declined, and the company decided to look into other avenues to make use of its engineering facilities.

The project was handed to Gunner Ljungstrom, who had gained experience of car design and manufacture with British companies Rover and Triumph. Given a clean sheet of paper to design a new car he developed a front-wheel-drive chassis driven by a vertical twin-cylinder engine. In another major departure from standard design practices of the time, he opted to make the engine a two-stroke rather than four-stroke design.

The car, known as the 92, was styled by Sason, who based his sleek bodyshell on the cross-section of an aircraft's wing. The result was a distinctive, aerodynamic saloon car with a long nose and a steeply raked tail.

Within weeks of its launch in 1950, the Saab 92 had won its first rally, and the company's long history of rally victories had begun. That first victory was in the Swedish Winter Rally, the car driven by Saab engineer Rolf Melde.

The 92 was joined by the 93 in 1956, which added a three-cylinder engine to the range but stayed with the original two-stroke concept. Hard on its heels came the 96, with a still larger engine. To gain the maximum economies of scale, Saab retained the same two-door body shell for all its models, irrespective of engine size, from 1950 until 1959. For the latter year it added an estate car to the range.

The rally side of the business was left in the hands of the ace driver Erik Carlsson. He campaigned the technically underpowered Saabs all over the world, winning numerous victories along the way. Among his earliest triumphs were outright wins in the Monte Carlo Rallies of 1962 and 1963.

By 1967 there were increasing clamours for Saab to adopt four-stroke power for their cars. Two-stroke engines of the day required oil to be mixed with their fuel, and offered no engine braking for descending hills. Four-stroke engines were seen as being easier and more conventional to drive.

Saab adopted the tough German Ford V4 engine in its 96 model from 1967. Sales soared, with over 20,000 of the new model being sold in that first year, while two-stroke sales fell to under 1,000. The valiant little two-stroke was discontinued in 1968, and the handsome original body style was dropped in 1968 to make way for the new 99 model.

In an attempt to break into the American sports-car market, Saab launched the curious Sonnet model in 1966. It was initially powered by the tuned two-stroke unit from the rally-derived 96 Sport model, with the V4 engine arriving in due course. The Sonnet was a small closed coupé with a sharp nose and a flat rear reminiscent of the TVRs of the day. Performance

Behind the Whee

was reasonable, but the retention of a column gearchange raised a few criticisms in the motoring press. Production lasted until 1974. Never a real sales success in the intended market, the Sonnet did find fame as a cult car wherever it was sold. As an alternative to the usual small British sports cars in America it was quieter, smoother and more civilized.

The new 99 was again designed by Sason, but this time power was from the British company Triumph. Engine development was an expensive process, and Saab approached Triumph to consider producing a new engine between them that they could both use, while development costs for both companies would be halved. The result was the single-overhead-camshaft four-cylinder engine that powered a whole generation of Saabs, and also saw service in the Triumph Dolomite and TR7 ranges.

Saab soon developed the engine in its own way, and from 1972 it had its own engine plant. Supplies of Triumph-built engines ceased in 1973. By this time Saab had also taken over the Scania truck company, and adopted its griffin badge for its cars.

The 99 was a lower, more 1970s-style design that would still look good by the time it was

replaced in 1984. By then it would have been stretched to create the Saab 900, and given birth to the rapid Saab 99 Turbo. Great measures were taken to make the cars solid and comfortable over long distances. Second only to Volvos, the later Saabs became renowned for their strength.

The last new Saab before financial troubles took hold was the 9000. One of what is known as the 'group-four' range, it was another joint development with other manufacturers to keep costs

Below left: Styled to follow aeroplane practice, Saab cars like this late-1950s 92B are invariably aerodynamic.

Above right: From the front, the early Saab models looked rather less graceful. Even so, the smooth, uncluttered lines of this 1956 92B show off its aircraft heritage.

Right: Saabs were soon used as the basis for racing cars after their early rally successes. Pictured is a Saab 94 from 1956.

Left: The original Saab badge clearly shows the company's origins as an aircraft manufacturer.

Below: The Sonnet sports car was only a moderate sales success, but soon became a cult car, especially in the American market. These two examples of the Sonnet II date from 1967/8.

to a minimum. The basic floorpan was shared with the Alfa Romeo 164, Lancia Dedra and Fiat Tempra, but each manufacturer fitted their own body and engine combination. That all four cars were sales successes surely indicates that the project was an effective one.

With debts in the car division mounting, Saab was acquired by General Motors in the late 1980s. They implemented reforms that cut the number of man-hours taken to build a new Saab by over two-thirds. The Saab range was starting to look dated by the early 1980s, and GM had the money to revitalize it. A new 900 was launched based on the Vauxhall/Opal Vectra floorpan, and larger GM engines were made available for other vehicles in the range. In addition to modernizing the Saab range, GM made use of Saab's surplus production capacity to build Calibras and Senators for the European markets.

As to the future, GM has been quoted in the press as saying they see Saab producing a range of its own cars for the foreseeable future, rivalling the likes of BMW, Mercedes and Jaguar. And who are we to argue with GM?

Skoda

Manufactured: 1895 to date.

The Name: The current company was named after Emil Skoda, whose engineering firm took over the original Laurin-Klement concern in 1925.

The Badge: The Skoda badge is based on a chrome flying arrow that was mounted on Skoda car bonnets during the 1930s.

History: The Skoda story started way back in 1895 when Vaclav Klement and Vaclav Laurin set up a bicycle-repair shop in Mlada Boleslav, near Prague, in what was then the Austro-Hungarian Empire. As with so many bicycle manufacturers of the time, their minds eventually turned to the manufacture of motor cars, although in their case they skipped the usual step of starting out with motorcycle production.

Their first vehicle, a light car called the Type A Voiturette, was launched in 1905. Marketed under the brand name of Laurin-Klement, as were all their early products, the Voiturette was a conventional twin-cylinder car with a top speed of some 30mph.

Cars with four cylinders followed, as did the powerful type FF with it's 4.8-litre eight-cylinder engine. With cars still facing an uncertain future, Laurin-Klement diversified into producing commercial vehicles and buses. In a sign of what was to come they also enjoyed a string of racing successes under the control of Otto Hyeronymus, a well-known racing driver who joined the company in 1908 with that sole aim in mind.

In 1925 the Skoda company, already well regarded for its heavy industrial work, purchased Laurin-Klement. For a while the cars carried both Skoda and Laurin-Klement badges, but the original name was soon dropped in favour of Skoda.

The first cars produced by the new company from 1924 to 1930 were licensed versions of contemporary Hispano-Suizas. For 1930, new models designed by Skoda itself were launched.

Above right: The Skoda 136 Black Rapid coupé of the 1980s — one of the first vehicles in the UK to offer fuel injection as standard.

Right: Skoda ancestor — a 1910 Laurin-Klement Type G tourer. Early Skodas were far removed from the utilitarian transport for which they later became known.

Available with four-, six- and eight-cylinder engines, they powered a wide range of cars from small economy vehicles to big limousines.

The smallest of these cars, the 900cc 420, was developed into Skoda's first widely known product, the Popular. Along with the larger Rapid and Superb models it made the Skoda name famous all over Europe, helped no doubt by the cars' widely-publicized successes in endurance rallies of the time. Skodas even appeared with some success in the Monte Carlo Rally.

In the middle of the opening battles of the Second World War, Skoda was forced by the German occupiers into war work, and the car-manufacturing division was split from the other parts of the group by the restored government in 1945. Under this new arrangement it became known as Automobilove Zavody Narodi Podnik (Automobile Works National Enterprise), or ANZP. This continued until 1948 when a Communist coup in Czechoslovakia saw the company nationalized and amalgamated again. Now made behind the Iron Curtain, Skodas would soon start to look old-fashioned by Western standards.

New models arrived in 1954 in the form of the 440 models. These were a handsome range of saloons and convertibles with the then fashionable column gearchange. Suspension was via a strange arrangement of swing axles front and rear, which could lead to some strange handling under energetic driving in anything other than ideal conditions. These were the first Skodas to display their long-standing trademark of low prices and good value for money, and many more would follow. The 440 was updated for 1958, and saw the first use of the Octavia and Felicia names recently revived on modern Skodas.

The car most people think of being the 'typical' Skoda arrived in 1964. Initially known as the 1000MB, it featured an advanced four-cylinder engine mounted in the rear of the vehicle. The strange swing-axle arrangement for the rear suspension was retained, and with the engine's weight at the rear it could lead to some 'interesting' handling in the hands of careless drivers. From a more charitable standpoint, the 1000MB offered the likes of reclining seats and an all-synchromesh gearbox at a price that made many other manufacturers envious.

These rear-engined cars would go on to make the Skoda name truly famous. Developed into the faster S110R coupés, they would become the poor man's sports coupé in many European countries. Introduced in 1970, they offered a willing 90mph and entertaining motoring for the price of a basic Ford Escort. Their rear-wing air vents and slightly strange engine note would make them instantly recognizable to a whole generation of motorists.

The range was redesignated and lightly redesigned as the Estelle in 1977. The evil-handling rear suspension was made worse by the extra power, and the car was completely

Behind the Wheel

rethought for 1979. Alloy wheels became standard for most markets, and budget rally cars were built by a number of car magazines to prove just what you could do with your Skoda. The detractors had been laughing for years, but the Estelle range offered outstanding value for money and perfectly adequate handling for all but the most demanding drivers. 1982 saw the arrival of a convertible version, and an updated Rapid coupé that would eventually go on to offer fuel injection for a bargain-basement price. It was even possible to buy a performance conversion that was widely praised in the motoring press, and which enabled Skoda owners happily to knock wheels with the hot hatches of the day.

Everything changed in 1989 when the new Favorit was launched. The advanced 1.3-litre engine was retained, but now it was fitted to a modern-looking hatchback body with the engine in the front. Suddenly the comedians stopped laughing. Styled by Bertone, it looked as up-to-date as most of the cars on Europe's roads, and all at the usual Skoda bargain price.

Volkswagen bought Skoda in 1993 and set about making it even more profitable. The Favorit was lightly restyled and renamed the Felicia, and for 1996 Skoda launched its largest car since the Second World War. The Octavia was a family-sized saloon car, powered by a wide range of engines from both the Skoda and VW stables. For the first time there was also a diesel in the range. The quality of construction had been raised to among the finest in Europe, and Skoda now offers its widest range since 1948.

Above left: The first Skoda Felicia was available as a handsome convertible. This example dates from 1959.

Above right: The Octavia saloon – this one a 1964 model – was a more basic version of the twin-carburettor Felicia model.

Below right: The Felicia saloon of the late 1950s and early 1960s was a handsome vehicle delivered at an affordable price.

Sunbeam

Manufactured: 1901 to 1976

The Name: There are many competing theories as to where the Sunbeam name originated from. One suggests that it was inspired by a line in a hymn that ran 'Sunbeams scorching all the day' – scorching being a slang term for driving fast. Another is that the cars were named after the yacht used by Lord and Lady Brassey in their famous round-the-world voyage.

The Badge: Early Sunbeams were badged with a design of the sun bursting through the clouds, with suitably prominent sunbeams.

History: John Marston, a dedicated bicycle enthusiast, started the Sunbeamland Cycle factory at Wolverhampton in 1887. Another of his family, Charles Marston, had founded the Villiers company in 1898 to produce bicycle components for other manufacturers. In the depths of the Villiers works an apprentice was quietly building the prototype of what would become the first Sunbeam car.

It emerged in 1901 in the form of the Sunbeam-Mabberly, the latter part of the name being its designer's surname. Powered by a De Dion engine, this first car could only be described as bizarre. It had four wheels, but instead of the usual 'wheel-at-each-corner' arrangement favoured by most cars, they were laid out in a diamond pattern, with a single wheel front and rear and a pair in the middle, allowing room for two passengers.

More conventional cars followed, and in 1905 the Sunbeam Motor Company was formed. After a number of management and directorial changes, a programme of competition was embarked upon to provide publicity, and sales soared between 1909 and 1913 on the back of it.

Sunbeam occupied its time during the First World War producing ambulances and aircraft engines, but with the return of peace, car production rose steadily. From its humble two-acre premises in 1905, Sunbeam now occupied a thirty-acre factory that could dealt with most of its own casting, machining and body work.

In 1920 Sunbeam was merged with Talbot/Darracq to form the larger STD Motors Ltd (Sunbeam, Talbot, Darracq). Sunbeam soon

Below left: The 3-litre Sunbeam-Talbot of 1925 was the first production car to use a twin-overhead-camshaft engine.

Right: The Sunbeam-Talbot 21hp Speed Model 4-door coupé of 1935. After the Second World War, Sunbeam-Talbots were relaunched with only minor styling tweaks until newer designs could be rushed into production, so a 1946 model would have been almost identical to this pre-war version.

became the sporting marque of the group, becoming ever-deeper involved with record-breaking and competition work. Malcolm Campbell used a Sunbeam-based car to take the World Speed Record at Pendine Sands in 1924, and in 1925 the first car to wear the Sunbeam Tiger name was unveiled. It was powered by a special engine made up of two supercharged straight-six units mounted on a common engine block to create a V12 engine. It set a record of 151.33mph at Southport Sands. Campbell's record of 1924 had stood at 146.57mph.

Away from the races, Sunbeam was making a name for itself producing fast, luxury touring cars using Talbot engines. Most notable was the sporting 3-litre of 1925. It was the first mass-production car to offer a twin-overhead-camshaft engine and set the technological pace for the cars around it.

Falling sales led to an end of the racing programme in 1926, and the big touring-car range was run down during the late 1920s and early 1930s. Sunbeam's expertise in the production of aero engines was also a victim of falling sales, and its last V12 offering found few buyers.

The Sunbeam name had a revival in 1929 when it became associated with a successful range of buses and trams that would sell well until the business was taken over by the Guy company in the aftermath of the Second World War.

A new small Sunbeam for 1934 was a modest success, but these were troubled times for the company. Sales were still dropping, and in 1931 the whole board had resigned over accusations of a lack of efficiency and poor organization.

The Rootes Group stepped in to rescue the Sunbeam name in 1935, and added it to its already impressive range of Hillman, Humber, Singer and Commer vehicles. The Sunbeam and Talbot names were joined, and a new light Sunbeam-Talbot was introduced based on the Hillman Minx of the time. It achieved passable sales before the Second World War brought production to a halt.

After the war, the Sunbeam-Talbot name was relaunched on a range of modern-looking saloons and convertibles under the 80 and 90 designations. A succession of ever larger Rootes-derived engines changed the car from an underpowered poser's vehicle when introduced, to a potent rally car with the final adoption of the 2.3-litre Humber Hawk engine; earlier versions had made do with the 1.6-litre Hillman Minx engine. Following successes in the Alpine Rally, the Mk3 convertible was renamed the Alpine for 1953, and the first of a range of sports cars was born.

It was all change in 1959 when the new Alpine arrived. Based, rather strangely, on the Hillman Husky estate car floorpan, the new Alpine was an up-to-date sports car powered by a tuned Minx engine. Unlike many of its contemporaries it committed the mortal sin of being a comfortable sports car, and so was widely regarded as being only for the 'soft' enthusiast. Nevertheless it was as fast as most of its competitors, especially when larger engines followed the early 1.5-litre unit. The styling was regularly updated, with the early model's fashionable fins quietly fading as the years passed.

As an answer to the criticisms of the Alpine's lack of performance, Rootes revived the Tiger

name for 1964. The idea was simple. Take one 1.6-litre Alpine, throw away the engine and fit a 4.2-litre (the American market got an even larger 4.7-litre unit) American Ford V8 engine. Result – the sort of power and exhaust note any self-respecting enthusiast should have killed for. Unfortunately, it still looked like an Alpine and sales were poor, despite *Autocar*'s rave reviews. When Chrysler took control of Rootes the car was quickly dropped, as the US giant could not be seen producing a car powered by one of its competitor's engines.

All through the 1960s the Hillman Minx-based Rapier carried the flag for the sporting family man. Its engine size grew along with its badge-engineered brethren, and there were rally successes in the early days. There were even up-market Sunbeam versions of the little Hillman Imp.

The last car to bear the Sunbeam name arrived in 1967. The running gear was taken from the Hillman Hunter, and the styling was lifted from the Plymouth Barracuda. It was designed to carry the Sunbeam name in the face of cars like the Ford Capri, and had both the performance and style to do it. Its sleek fastback body offered full seating for four in a stylish pillarless bodyshell. But somewhere along the way the marketing went awry, and the Rapier died quietly in 1976.

...the new *Sunbeam* MK III

The Sunbeam name also died in 1976, then was promptly revived as a model name by Chrysler in 1977 on a Hillman Avenger-based hatchback. Uninspiring in standard form, the Sunbeam went on to grow teeth as the rapid but noisy Ti model, and to win the World Rally Championship in 1980 powered by a 2.2-litre Lotus engine. This car, the Talbot (Chrysler had gone by now) Sunbeam Lotus, saw limited production as a rapid road car. When it was put out of production in 1981, the sporting Sunbeam name had finally died, though it had gone out with a bang, not a whimper.

Left: The Sunbeam-Talbot Ten – this is a 1946 model – joined the previously separate names under the auspices of the Rootes Group in 1935.

Above right: Advertisement from 1954.

Below right: The 1950s Sunbeam-Talbot 80 and 90 cars were renamed as Alpines after successes in the Alpine Rally.

Triumph

Manufactured: 1923 to 1984

The Name: The Triumph name was chosen to be easily recognizable in any language.

The Badge: Most Triumphs carry a globe badge, symbolizing their position as a worldwide marque. A Standard-Triumph shield was used during the 1950s, and the final Triumphs wore a winner's-garland badge to commemorate the victories of the TR7 V8 rally cars.

History: Like many of the early manufacturers, Triumph first made bicycles in 1887, followed by motorcycles in 1902, and eventually turned to motor cars in 1923. The first Triumph was the 10/20 model, which grew into the 13/35 for 1925; a fast 2.2-litre tourer joined the range in 1927. These were all conventional cars, widely praised in the press for their standard of equipment and quality of construction. The car that was to establish the Triumph name, however, arrived in 1928: the Super Seven. Aimed squarely at the luxury end of the Austin Seven market, the Super Seven sold well in many guises. Larger models followed

STANDARD VANGUARD

*A pleasure to drive . . . .
economical to run*

The Standard Motor Co. Ltd. Coventry. London: Standard House, 37 Davies St. Grosvenor Sq. W.1
Standard Cars   Standard Commercial Vehicles   Ferguson Tractors   Triumph Cars

before the Triumph marque started to show a move towards the sporting end of the market.

The Southern Cross sports cars were faster than many of their competitors, and offered standards of comfort MG drivers could only dream about. The sports models were supported by a range of fast touring cars under the 'Gloria' banner, which made use of a wide range of engines and no fewer than three chassis styles. Once again the motoring press said friendly things about the Gloria, and journalists had even fewer reservations about the performance of their replacements, the Dolomite range.

When introduced in 1933 the Dolomites were fitted with a 'waterfall'-style chrome grille after the American fashion of the time. Flanked by two prominent chrome air-horns the grille dominated the front of the car, and drivers either loved or loathed it. The fact that it was quietly deleted on the following Vitesse model, which was essentially similar to the Dolomite, rather speaks for itself.

Donald Healey was a prominent presence at Triumph during the 1930s, and he was responsible for the famous supercharged Triumph Dolomite straight-eight. Based closely on the Alfa Romeo 2300 of the time, it was to have been the basis of a very fast production car after proving

itself in competition. In the face of financial constraints Healey himself decided to drive the car in the Monte Carlo Rally, and would no doubt have made a good showing had he not collided

---

Is That Really True?

The 1950s Triumph Roadster would go on to find fame as Detective Bergerac's car in the BBC TV series of the same name, set on Jersey. The car now resides at Jersey Goldsmiths in St Ouens, Jersey.

The Triumph Herald was named after a boat belonging to one of the company's directors.

A four-door version of the Triumph Herald saw long service in India, where it was manufactured and badged as the Standard Gazelle.

The Herald family gave birth to a German amphibious vehicle called the 'Amphicar'. Few were built, and those that did find buyers suffered badly from rust and salt corrosion when their owners tried using them in the sea.

with a train in thick fog and written the car off before even reaching the start. Pictures of the time show the car practically destroyed, and Healey lucky to have survived. The project was cancelled after only three cars and six engines had been built.

By this time the Triumph range had become large and rambling, with small family cars, fast tourers and luxury saloons all fighting for customers. In the face of falling sales Triumph, having already sold their motorcycle wing to finance expansion, were faced with receivership. They were bought out by an engineering company, largely for their production space.

After the Second World War broke out in 1939, the Triumph works were given over to the production of aircraft fuselages, notably for the De Havilland Mosquito and the Bristol Beaufighter. The Coventry blitz of 14 November 1940, which killed more than 1,000 people and destroyed the city's medieval cathedral and many other buildings, also destroyed the Triumph factories, and

their owners sold the company's name and reputation (there was little else to sell) to Captain John Black of Standard Motors.

Black had arrived at Standard in the 1920s having made his name at Hillman. He had been responsible for the famous 'Flying Standard' range of aerodynamic cars and was a keen supporter of the wartime 'shadow-factory' scheme. Under this, every factory producing war materials had a 'shadow' that could take over its operation should the original be destroyed. Once the war was over Standard retained their new 'shadow' factories and looked around for work to fill them. As a result, a contract was signed with Harry Ferguson to build his revolutionary new tractor design. These were small, efficient vehicles that were the first to offer a hydraulic drive from the rear to power farm machinery; previously, most farm machines had required an individual dedicated power source to drive them. Ferguson's design was an instant success and many of these tractors are still in service all over the world. It also introduced a compact 4-cylinder engine to Standard-Triumph that would soon see service in a very different role.

In the face of increasing competition in the sporting market, Black had been looking for a sporting marque to give the Standard image a boost, and had already tried and failed to buy both Riley and SS/Jaguar. With nothing left of the pre-war Triumphs to work with, he was free to design a whole new range based on established Standard components.

Built with techniques learned during the company's aircraft-production days, the first post-war Triumphs were the famous 'razor-edge' models. This was a range of traditionally styled saloons with sharp edges to the bodywork at a time when other manufacturers were turning towards soft curves. The cars were well equipped and well made, but even the largest 2-litre models lacked performance. Top of the line was the bulbous Roadster model. Designed as a fast tourer, it was one of the last production cars to make use of the 1930s 'dicky-seat' system offering two extra seats covered by a closing panel in the tail. The panel opened to allow the passengers in, then stayed folded forwards to form a simple windscreen. Styling was a throwback to the pre-war era and the cars were never a sales success.

The Roadster did, however, lend its initials to perhaps the most famous Triumph range in 1953. The Triumph Roadster was the original TR, and in 1953 the TR2 arrived - the cheap sports car that Captain Black hoped would take America by storm. Powered by the Ferguson

Above left: A 1938 Triumph Super Seven. The Super Seven established the Triumph name from its launch in 1928.

Right: Introduced in 1970, the inspired Stag provided effortless long-distance touring, but was killed off by poor build quality, which seriously affected reliability.

Tractor 2-litre engine (which was also seeing service in the Standard Vanguard saloon), it offered basic sporting driving at a sensible price. An instant sales success, updated TR3 and 3A models quickly followed. The range was totally restyled and made more comfortable with the TR4 of 1961, and three years later gained independent rear suspension as the TR4A, while a six-cylinder engine from the big Triumph saloons equipped the TR5 of 1967. Its successor a year later, the TR6, was the first mass-produced British car to boast fuel injection as a standard fitting, although inexperienced mechanics the world over tended to curse it, for the Lucas system was widely regarded as being more trouble than it was worth. American emissions laws forced export models to retain conventional carburettors, and many who owned these felt they were lucky.

A lack of space at Triumph during the 1950s led to problems when it came to designing and building their new small car. This was intended to replace the ageing Standard 8/10 range, already being marketed as Triumphs in the vital American market. The novel solution to the problem was to return to the old-fashioned method of separate-chassis construction, the intention being to have all the sections made by separate suppliers, and then bolt them together at final assembly. The result was the Triumph Herald.

The side-effect of this method of construction was that it made it very easy to produce different versions of the vehicle. Simply by using a different roof section, the saloon could be made into a coupé, convertible and estate car. By mixing and matching engines and body styles it formed the basis of the six-cylinder Vitesse range, the Spitfire sports car, and the GT6 coupé, and the last of the range was in production until 1980 in the form of the Spitfire 1500. Although widely regarded as a backward step at the time, the fact that this production method remained in use for so long rather answers its critics for itself.

The only major criticism levelled at the Herald-based cars by the press was their basic swing-axle suspension system, which was prone to cause breakaway at the rear wheels in extreme driving conditions. The problem was addressed on later models, but somehow the Herald never lost its reputation for going backwards through hedges in the hands of inexperienced drivers. However, its well-earned reputation for manoeuvrability and its amazingly tight turning circle made it a firm favourite with driving schools.

The image of the luxury Triumphs was upheld by the 2000 and 2500 range. These big saloon cars were well regarded by their owners, not least because they offered effortless performance from their 6-cylinder engines. Designed to be sold in direct competition to the big Rovers, they became somewhat of an embarrassment when both companies came under the British Leyland umbrella in the 1960s.

In common with most British car companies, things started to go wrong for Triumph in the 1970s. A big luxury tourer, the Stag, was launched in 1970 to a rapturous reception. Things turned bad very quickly, however, when it was found that its new V8 engine (prototypes had used the well proven straight-six engine) was fragile and frequently poorly assembled; indeed, specialists taking the engines apart in later years were amazed to find casting sand left in the engines during production. The massive sales envisaged never materialized, and the model was allowed to die quietly in 1977.

The British Leyland group had taken control of Triumph in the late 1960s, at a time when the whole group suffered from labour-relations problems. Strikes were common, and by the mid-1970s build quality was at an all-time low. The new TR7 model of 1975 and the Dolomite range that had replaced the Heralds were all good, solid cars let down by the way they were built. TR7s developed a reputation for total electrical failure, and the remarkable 16-valve Dolomite Sprint was seen as troublesome because dealerships appeared not to know how to maintain the engine. In the face of falling sales the inspired Rover-engined 3.5-litre TR8 never even made it into volume production, despite publicity generated by the rally team's efforts.

The Triumph name was not allowed to die with dignity when the Dolomite and the Spitfire were dropped in 1980. It was resurrected on the first car to arrive as part of the new Rover/Honda co-operation. The Triumph Acclaim was little more than a badge-engineered Honda Ballade, and no one mourned when production ceased in 1984. The Triumph name died with it.

TVR

Manufactured: 1949 to date.

The Name: The name is made up of letters taken from the founder's Christian name. He was TreVoR Wilkinson.

The Badge: All TVRs bear those initials somewhere on their bodywork.

History: Born in 1923, Trevor Wilkinson set up Trevcar Motors after spending time in the forces during the Second World War. A trained mechanic, by 1947 he had entered into partnership with Jack Picard to form TVR Engineering. Initially producing a selection of specials and competition cars to each customer's specific requirements, they moved on to producing complete cars in kit form from 1953.

Moves to produce a series production run of a TVR-designed car called the Jomar for the United States looked promising to the small Blackpool-based company. It expanded fast, but in 1958 it was forced into receivership as it overreached its finances. Layton Sportscars took over briefly, with the company passing on to a pair of TVR dealers in 1961, and Grantura Plastics took control for 1962. These irregular gaps in production brought the fledgeling Jomar project to an untimely end.

The only product from 1958 was the handsome Grantura coupé, named after the company that supplied the body shell. The running gear was a mixture of Ford and BMC, and a wide selection of engines were available – from the humble Ford side-valve, through the MGA unit and on to the frantic Coventry-Climax engine. Superchargers were even available for some engines. Crude but effective, the light TVRs found fame as cheap competition cars.

American TVR dealer Jack Griffith ordered engineless bodies, fitted them with big American Ford V8 engines and marketed them in the United States as Griffiths. From 1963 some started to find their way back to the UK.

Below: TVR Tasmin 280i fixed-head coupé from the 1980s. In an effort to build a budget TVR, the 2.8-litre engine from the Ford Capri was used in place of the usual 3.5-litre Rover V8.

Above right: The wedge shaped, Rover-V8 powered TVRs of the 1980s, like this 350i convertible, epitomized the styling of the era.

Below right: The Tuscan/Griffith-styled cars of the 1990s not only looked and sounded good, but performed well.

The range was rationalized and updated for 1967 with the launch of the Vixen. Basically the same as the Grantura, it now featured the Cortina GT engine as standard and a number of other Ford touches on the exterior such as the rear lights. The interior was far more luxurious than what had gone before, and ordinary drivers at last had a TVR they could drive to work every day.

The Tuscan range was updated for 1969 with the option of a British Ford 3-litre V6 in place of the American Ford 4.7-litre V8. Running gear was now all Ford Cortina-derived and alloy wheels became a standard fitment.

The whole range was updated into the M series for 1971. The basic style was retained, but power could now be had from a range of Triumph engines as well as the usual Ford units. Build quality and comfort were much improved, while the basic styling remained the same until the launch of the angular Tasmin in 1980.

Gone were the curves of the M series, and in came a sharply angular design from the same pen that had created the 1970s Lotus range. The chassis was very similar to the M-series cars, only now it wore Jaguar rear suspension and had been stretched to accommodate the projected new engines. Early models used the Ford V6, and occasionally the Ford 4-cylinder, but the Rover V8 engine soon took over.

to date, featuring the sort of performance that could worry even the most expensive exotic.

All the big wedge-shaped TVRs had two things in common – performance and price. They were fast, and expensive. In an attempt to capture the hearts and wallets of less well-off motorists, TVR launched the S3 for 1986. Back came the curvy styling that had been so popular in the 1960s and 1970s, and power was from the old Ford V6 engine.

The current range arrived in 1988 with the new Tuscan. Featuring a stylish body very loosely based on the earlier M-series cars, it was powered by a mighty 4.4-litre version of the Rover V8. Top speed was 165mph, and 0-60 came up in 3.7 seconds. Initially designed as a racing car, the Tuscan went on to give birth to the Griffith of the 1990s, and from then on the Chimaera and the closed Cerbera models. Engines ranged from 3.9 to a full 5 litres, and all models produced perhaps the most beautiful exhaust note ever to have graced a British road car. With sales rising steadily, TVR goes from strength as one of the tiny number of car manufacturers who can still claim to be all British. Lots more of the same is clearly the order of the day.

Names were dropped for the 1984 season in favour of the Ford V6-engined 280 (2.8-litre engine) and the 350 (3.5-litre Rover V8). The Rover engine was enlarged to create the 400, 420 and 450 models. The latter was the fastest TVR

Above left: The powerhouse of the current TVR range, the much enlarged Rover V8. Some TVRs use it in 4.4-litre form.

Below left: A TVR 350i in it's natural habitat, the wide-open road.

Below right: Introduced in 1911, the Prince Henry was Vauxhall's first famous design, and was regarded a one of the finest cars available at the time. The example here dates from 1914.

Vauxhall

Manufactured: 1903 to date.

The Name: The company was named after the original location of its factory, Vauxhall in London. The actual area name is derived from the term 'Vaux's Manor', 'manor' also being an old English word for a hall. Vaux was Faukes de Breaute, who built a manor in the area in the thirteenth century.

The Badge: The griffin was the badge of Faukes de Breaute. It has also been adopted as the symbol of Vauxhall council, and can still be seen in the ironwork on Vauxhall Bridge.

History: The company that would become known as Vauxhall Cars was first known as the Vauxhall Iron Works in 1857. It was initially known for its marine engines, and its first car appeared in 1903. It was a simple, two-seater vehicle powered by a single-cylinder engine. Despite using the then common tiller steering, it also featured an advanced coil-spring suspension system when other manufacturers were still using cart springs.

The company moved to Luton, Bedfordshire, in 1905, and there it has remained to this day. In the same year it made a leap up-market from its basic 6hp models with a 3.3-litre car. This was a big, fast touring machine, soon developed into the famous Prince Henry model for 1911. This was a full four-seater that featured the fluted bonnet which would remain a symbol of the marque well into the 1950s. In its day the Prince Henry was regarded as being one of the finest cars available. A tuned 4-litre version of the same engine found its way into Grand Prix cars, the finest of which produced some 130bhp.

During the First World War, Vauxhall produced 25hp tourers for the armed forces, and its earlier range was resurrected after the war. In the depressed economic climate sales were slow for such expensive cars, despite the publicity generated by the company's racing enterprises.

Mounting losses brought Vauxhall to the brink of receivership before it was rescued by America's General Motors in 1925. GM liked what it saw amongst the up-market Vauxhall cars, but forced the company to look at the lower end of the market to support its larger vehicles.

The first car launched by Vauxhall after the GM takeover was the 20/60, closely followed in 1927 by the six-cylinder Cadet model (a name that was passed to another GM subsidiary, Opel, for later cars). Larger six-cylinder models were introduced to appeal to wealthier buyers who wanted something more than basic cars but could not afford to venture into the upper Vauxhall range.

The advanced Vauxhall Ten arrived in 1937. This was the first Vauxhall to make use of the new monocoque construction methods, and featured an efficient overhead-valve engine when many of the opposition were still using side-valves. Performance was lively for such a small car, and it was partnered by the far larger Twenty-Five models until the Second World War brought developments to an end. Immediately prior to hostilities, however, all Vauxhalls were fitted with hydraulic brakes for the 1939 season – a major advance over the partially cable- and rod-operated systems in use by most manufacturers of the time.

During the war, Vauxhall manufactured ammunition, and later produced the Churchill tank. With the coming of peace, the company joined the other major manufacturers in restarting production of its pre-war range until the 1948 Motor Show.

The new cars clearly showed the American influence of Vauxhall's parent company in their styling, with full-width chrome radiator grilles and plenty of supporting brightwork. Two cars were based on the same basic body, the four-cylinder Wyvern and the six-cylinder Velox. Both were heavy designs, and the smaller Wyvern's engine struggled. But both sold in respectable

Is That Really True?

Prior to taking over Vauxhall, GM had been looking to buy into the British car market by buying Austin, but after problems with the latter's shareholders it jumped at the chance to buy Vauxhall.

The first Wyvern/Velox range had windscreen wipers driven directly by the rotation of the engine, not by an electric motor. Compared with those of the Ford vacuum-operated system, they were wonderful.

The F-type Victors rusted at such a rate that for a time Canada actually halted imports.

Early Vauxhall Viva GTs had rather eccentric exhaust pipes that boasted no fewer than four tailpipes.

When the F-type Victor was launched every dealership was issued with a set of 3D glasses and slides so customers could view every possible colour and trim combination before making up their minds.

The last of the Victor line, the FE, was to live on in India until 1997 as the Hindustan Contessa. It grew large bumpers to suit the local driving conditions, but was otherwise instantly recognizable.

enough numbers for Vauxhall to update the range for 1951. The mechanics remained largely the same, but there was a new, far sleeker body style based on the 1949 Chevrolet range.

In the face of the famous Ford Zephyr/Zodiac models, Vauxhall launched the gaudy Cresta in 1954. This offered two-tone paint inside and out, and such luxuries as a leather interior, a heater as standard, and fashionable rear-wheel spats. Later models could even be specified with three-tone paintwork.

All was swept away in 1957 with the F-type Victor. Based heavily on the styling of the 1955 Chevrolet range, it was one of the first British cars to offer a wrap-round windscreen (even if the bottom corner stuck out over the door area and could cripple the knees of unwary passengers as they got in and out). There was chrome everywhere, and the exhaust pipe exited through a hole in the rear bumper. The Victor offered brisk performance, a stylish presence on the road – and rusted. Rust-proofing was in its infancy in the 1950s, and the F-type rotted quickly. Few examples survive today, which is a shame for a car that should be regarded as being as much part of the 1950s as the more fondly remembered Fords. The Victor name lived through until 1972, however, with each successive restyling making them more anonymous on the road.

The 'big' Vauxhall name was kept alive by the Cresta range, an enlarged Victor with a six-cylinder engine. Aimed at the Rover market, the Cresta (and an up-market Velox version) died out quietly in the late 1960s, their six-cylinder engine passing on to the sporting versions of the Victor.

Buyers of smaller cars were catered for with the Viva HA of 1963. Essentially a re-badged version of the German Opel Cadet, the van version lived well into the 1980s, and will be for ever remembered in Britain as the British Gas

van. For its time, it offered reasonable performance and refinement. Later and much developed HB and HC models of the car would actually have hot GT and 'Brabham'-tuned versions in their ranges. These developed quite a name for themselves on the race tracks of the time, and the last of the range, the HC, went on to be the basis of the popular Chevette model.

A fire-breathing 2.3-litre version of the Viva HC wore a sporting coupé body shell and the name Magnum. Built to face up to the Ford Escort RS2000, it was more than up to the task, but relatively few found buyers.

The 1970s were successful years for Vauxhall, and its best-selling Cavalier and Chevette models became familiar sights on the road. By the 1980s most Vauxhalls were actually designed and built by GM plants all over the world. The little Nova hatchback was built in Spain, and was sold in mainland Europe as the Corsa. The big Vauxhall Carlton was also known as the Opel Senator, and almost all traces of Vauxhall's independence had vanished.

British Vauxhall had one last fling with the gloriously excessive Lotus Carlton. An uprated Carlton was fitted with a Lotus-developed engine and suspension system to render it capable of over 170mph and a 0-60 time of 5.2 seconds, while still offering generous and comfortable seating for four people. Wide wheels and vast wheel arches gave the game away to onlookers, but few could even come close to catching one when it was on the move. Unfortunately, it was launched during one of Britain's periodic 'ban all fast cars' phases in the press and sales were slow. Nice try, guys. Some of us appreciated it.

Behind the Wheel

Volkswagen

Manufactured: 1936 to date.

The Name: German *Volkswagen*, or more precisely *Volks Wagen*, translates as 'people's car'.

The Badge: The Volkswagen badge is a simple display of the initial letters of the words making up the company name, within a circle.

History: The Volkswagen (VW) project was one of Adolf Hitler's grand plans when he came to power. Vast numbers of new roads were being built in Germany as a symbol of the country's new industrial age, and Hitler believed every family of the German People (hence people's car) should be able to afford a car to drive along them. He decreed that a car should be designed and built to allow this to happen. The Führer also felt that motor racing was the fastest way to improve the technology available to his engineers, and in the 1930s the German Auto-Union team was unbeatable on the Grand Prix tracks of Europe. The team was funded by the German Government, and the cars were designed, developed and built irrespective of the costs involved.

Hitler found an unlikely ally in Ferdinand Porsche, a talented German engineer whose work would lead to a range of small sports cars bearing his name after the Second World War. Porsche had long wanted to build a small, efficient car that anyone could afford to buy, but his earlier designs of a similar concept for motorcycle makers Zundapp and NSU had come to nothing. Hitler's target was for a car that could be put on sale for under 1,000 Deutschmarks, less than half the price of the cheapest car on Germany's roads at the time.

In 1934 Porsche was given a year to design a new car, backed by the body controlling the now nationalized motor industry in Germany. Their backing was so inefficient that Porsche elected to build the first of his prototype cars at his own workshops. Furthermore, firms like Opel were openly against his plans, feeling their Kadett model was built as cheaply as it was possible to go and still produce a 'real' car.

The first car was finished in October 1936. Despite early plans to use a two-stroke engine, the car emerged with the basics of the now instantly recognizable flat four-cylinder air-cooled engine. It was extensively tested, and Hitler pronounced it suitable for production in early 1937.

Hitler himself laid the foundation stone at the Fallerslaben factory, and chose the name KDF-Wagen (from the Nazi slogan *'Kraft durch Freude'* – strength through joy) for the new car. A town was built specially for the workers at the new factory, and would be called Kraft Durch Freude Stadt (Strength Through Joy Town) after the Nazi movement of the time. While all this was going on, Porsche toured America to examine their production-line assembly methods to make his factory as efficient as possible.

The new car, soon known as the Beetle despite Hitler's proclamation, was sold on a type of hire-purchase system. Germans opened

The Beetle.

accounts in a stamp-saving scheme to buy the cars in instalments. When they had amassed sufficient stamps, they were entitled to collect a new car. Over 350,000 such accounts were opened before the Second World War began and the Beetle was put on hold, after fewer than 250 examples had been made.

KDF-Stadt was renamed Wolfsberg by the occupying British forces after the war, but despite offering the factory to several Allied nations, no one wanted it. It had been thoroughly bombed, and only one British officer, Major Ivan Hirst, showed any inclination to make anything of the existing works. With some reconstruction he had production running again by late 1945, building nearly 2,000 vehicles for military use. After more

reconstruction work, over 11,000 cars were produced in 1946.

The company was handed back to German control in 1948, and in 1949 the first Beetles were exported to America. VW never looked back as its sales rocketed. The company took great care to ensure there was a dealer network in place in America to sell its cars, and that there were adequate supplies of spares to meet any problems that might arise. The Beetle convertible, introduced in 1949, found a ready market in the sunshine states.

Many Germans who had paid into the savings scheme before the war were demanding discounts on the new cars, or in some cases even free cars. Cases were still running through the

Behind the Wheel

German courts well into the 1960s, depriving the company of much-needed development capital.

Overseas plants to build Beetles under licence quickly sprang up in Brazil, Australia, and America. Sales were expanded by the introduction of a succession of larger engines, and in 1954 the stylist Karmann started production of a sleek coupé called the Karmann Ghia. Although never the sales success of the Beetle convertible, its sleek lines and sporting looks made it another cult car in America. Beetle production was still riding on a high, and the 'people's car' was also joined by other saloons based on the same basic design.

By 1969 the rear-engined designs were starting to look dated and Fiat had overtaken VW as Europe's largest manufacturer. The conventional K70 saloon was launched in 1971, but few sold. It was not a bad car, but people both expected VWs to be rear-engined air-cooled cars, and at the same time criticized the company for building them. For a while VW could do no right in the eyes of the press and public. On the credit side, the 15 millionth Beetle was produced in 1972, and the 20 millionth would roll off the Mexico production line in 1981.

Opel overtook VW as Germany's largest car producer in 1971, despite the latter having swallowed Audi and NSU in the late 1960s. The new Passat arrived in 1973, a badge-engineered version of the Audi 80, but their next big success would not arrive until 1974.

The VW Golf, and its coupé brother the Sirocco, launched VW back into the best-seller charts again. They were tightly styled hatchbacks whose concept many other manufacturers would scramble to follow. Booted saloons had been the fashion until the Golf came along (even though the neglected Austin Maxi had featured a hatch since 1970). The new VW offered seating for four in comfort, front-wheel drive, and in 1976 gave the world the GTi badge. The hatchback world never looked back. The GTi offered sports-car performance in a practical hatchback body for the family. The already ailing two-seater sports-car market rolled over and died within a few years, with its cheaper offerings largely ignored in favour of the new GTi-class cars. After all, who

Above: The Golf – this is the Driver version – launched the initials 'GTi' on an unsuspecting world.

wanted to have to struggle with a hood in the rain when you could have a warm and dry but sporty car in all weathers?

The Golf was joined by the smaller Polo, and in time the larger Passat. Engines were steadily developed and increased, and all models received the customary periodic restyling touches at regular intervals. As the 1980s moved into the 1990s VW embarked on a programme of buying up smaller manufacturers. It took over Spanish SEAT, Czech Skoda and (unbelievably) British Bentley. Now the fourth-largest car manufacturer in the world behind Ford, GM and Toyota, VW looks as if it can afford to be optimistic as it moves into the twenty-first century.

Is That Really True?

Despite his passion to build cars for the German people, Hitler never actually learned to drive.

In America, the VW Golf is sold as the VW Rabbit.

The 1990s VW people carrier, the Sharan, is the same vehicle as the Ford Galaxy and the SEAT Alhambra. Development and production costs were shared to improve profitability.

Volvo

Manufactured: 1927 to date.
The Name: *Volvo* is Latin for 'I roll'.
The Badge: The Volvo badge is now the chemical symbol for iron with 'Volvo' lettered across it.
History: The Volvo marque was founded in 1927 by Assar Gabrielsson and Gustav Larson. The duo developed the idea for the company over a meal of crayfish in 1924. Their intention was to produce vehicles better suited to the Scandinavian climate than those currently available by utilizing high-quality steel for the bodies and buying-in the best available components for the rest of the car.

At the time, Gabrielsson was the sales manager of the Swedish bearing company SKF, which Larson joined in 1920 after spending some time with the British White and Pope engineering company.

Below: The PV544 range was the first to exhibit the Volvo trademarks of solidity and longevity, and the car was a sales success.

Gabrielsson personally financed the building of the first group of prototypes, which were styled by the Swedish artist Helmer Mas-Olle. Pentaverken, a well-known shipping engineering company, supplied the engines.

SKF were impressed by the prototypes produced privately by their staff, and agreed to fund manufacture of the first 1,000 production examples. They also allowed the duo to make use of one of their registered trademarks: AB Volvo. The name had originally been used by a subsidiary company that specialized in the production of ball bearings – hence the Latin 'I roll'.

The car was first shown to the world in 1927, and was christened the Jakob. The original plan had been to produce 500 of those first 1,000 cars as convertibles, and the remaining 500 as closed saloons. Given the extremes of cold encountered in Sweden it should come as no surprise to learn that in the end only 200 of the cars were produced as convertibles, the rest being delivered as the closed version.

A bigger six-cylinder engine was added to the range for 1929, and a range of trucks and taxis were introduced in 1928. Until the Second World

Behind the Wheel

Above: The P1800 model was made famous by Roger Moore in the 1960s television series *The Saint*. The story would have been very different, however, if Jaguar hadn't refused the loan of an E-Type.

War, Volvo commercial vehicles easily outsold their cars.

The briefly fashionable 'airflow' design style arrived at Volvo in 1936 in the form of the PV36 Carioca. Heavily influenced by the Chrysler Airflow, it was a sales success by Volvo's standards, while the Chrysler was one of the American giant's few failures.

Volvo cars became independent in 1935, and continued to show a healthy profit through the war years. As Sweden remained neutral, car manufacture continued all through the hostilities, even though production fell to fewer than a hundred cars a year.

The all-new PV444 was the first Volvo to find fame around the world. It was also the first to be officially exported to the vast American market, and once the Second World War had passed it soon made a name for itself as a rally car. It was a modern design, with independent front suspension and coil springs in place of the more commonly used cart springs at the rear. The earlier styling

cues could be seen in the large, bulbous front wings, but as a styling package it was neat and compact. This was the Volvo that started to make the name synonymous with toughness and longevity. Estates and vans followed as car production at last outstripped truck sales in the post-war years.

1956 saw the arrival of the most popular Volvo to date. Officially known as the Amazon only in Sweden for copyright reasons, the 121 saloon was nevertheless unofficially known by the name all over the world. Production would last until 1970, and it made the Volvo reputation for solid construction and indestructible mechanics into a legend. Styling was inspired by the Chrysler range of 1955, and the mechanics were largely based on the earlier PV444 range.

From 1960 to 1972, Volvo made a radical departure from their reliable but uninspiring saloons with the P1800. The mechanics were derived from the Amazon range, but the body was a sporty coupé with a large radiator grille, slim but prominent rear fins and fashionable double bumpers at the front. Assembled by Jensen in England, it was made instantly famous by Roger Moore in the TV version of *The Saint* after

Above: The Volvo 121 was better known as the Amazon, despite copyright rules forcing the name to be changed outside Sweden. This being a publicity photo, the number plate actually shows the car's date.

Jaguar refused the loan of an E-Type. It offered a sporting drive that owners of Volvo saloons could only dream about. Fuel injection was standard from 1968, and there was even an unusual estate car for the last year of production.

The first of the big square Volvos so well known today arrived in the form of the 140 in 1966, the same year as the millionth Volvo (a 120 saloon) was produced. It was joined by a six-cylinder version, the 164, for 1968, and by 1970 the Amazon was no more. Surplus P1800 engines found their way into some of the last of the two-

door Amazons to create the potent 123GT, a rare car treasured by owners today.

The 140 range gave birth to the block-sided estate cars so well known today, and for 1974 they were renamed the 240 range. These would go on to become the best-selling Volvos ever. They all wore big, heavy bumpers and offered a good ride over all but the worst terrain. They would find favour with antiques dealers and horse-box owners everywhere in Europe, and the larger models that came later took their styling cues from the 240 range for many years.

Volvo began working with the Dutch company DAF in 1968, and had taken control by 1974. DAF's main claim to fame was their rather strange hatchback, which was the only car on the

Behind the Whee

market to offer a form of automatic gearbox with infinitely variable drive ratios (they called it Variomatic). As this worked through a system employing what were effectively reinforced rubber bands, the cars had a reputation for fragility if neglected, and downright unreliability in their old age. Everyone laughed at the time when they suddenly appeared with Volvo badges in place of their original DAF insignia, but now technology has caught up with the idea. Today most of the major car manufacturers are using a similar system.

Volvo used their plant to build their smaller 340 series saloons, some of which made use of the DAF gearbox system. While an uninspiring car to drive or look at, the front-engine, rear-gearbox design offered good weight distribution and acceptable roadholding for a family saloon.

Volvo started to lose its way in the late 1980s. Their cars were getting larger, and commonly began to sport such excessive devices as heated steering wheels. Nice gimmicks, perhaps, but they made the cars heavy and expensive. The uninspiring 340 was replaced by the wedge-

shaped 440 and 480 range. The 440 was another dull-looking saloon, although at least the 480 looked like a fast, fun, sporty car. Poor build quality and an uninspiring Renault engine put an end to any chance of the latter being a sales success, and Volvo started to show losses for the first time by the early 1990s.

They confounded their critics by launching the 850 T-5. It wore the usual ultra-conventional Volvo estate-car body, but was powered by a new five-cylinder engine fitted with a potent

Left: 'Big and square' became the trademarks of Volvo cars all through the 1970s and 1980s, as this Turbo saloon demonstrates.

Below: Beloved of antique dealers everywhere, the 140/240 became Volvo's longest-selling model range.

turbocharger. Despite the road-safety groups protesting, sales soared. The British police found it to be the ideal motorway patrol car with its vast load-carrying area and effortless performance.

Volvo even had the nerve to enter a team of estate cars in the British Touring Cars race series and made a spirited showing against far sportier-looking vehicles. These were eventu-ally replaced by saloon and coupé designs, but for a while it really was possible to see estate cars knocking bumpers with the finest racing saloons of the day.

The Volvo range has now been largely over-hauled, and aside from their prominent grille they have taken on a new, smoother look for the new century. The company looks set for a renaissance.

Behind the Wheel